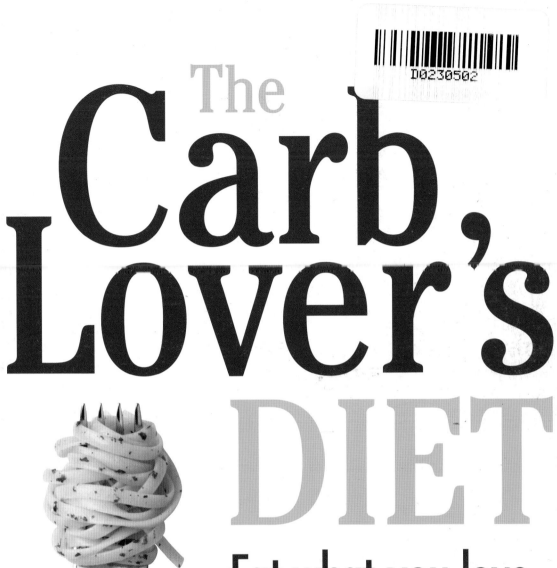

The Carb, Lover's DIET

Eat what you love & get slim for life

By **Ellen Kunes,** Editor in Chief,
& **Frances Largeman-Roth,**
of **Health** © magazine

©2010 Time Home Entertainment Inc.
135 West 50th Street, New York, NY 10020

This edition published 2010 by Hamlyn
a division of Octopus Publishing Group Ltd,
Endeavour House, 189 Shaftesbury Avenue, London, WC2H 8JY
www.octopusbooks.co.uk

An Hachette UK Company
www.hachette.co.uk

This book is intended as a general reference only, and is not to be
used as a substitute for medical advice or treatment. We urge you
to consult a doctor regarding any individual medical conditions or
specific health-related issues or questions.

ISBN 13:   978-0-6006-2325-0

A CIP catalogue record for this book is available
from the British Library.

Printed and bound in China

10 9 8 7 6 5 4 3 2 1

HEALTH MAGAZINE
Editor in Chief: Ellen Kunes
Creative Director: Ben Margherita
Design Director: José Fernandez

OCTOPUS PUBLISHING GROUP

Publishing Director: Stephanie Jackson
Managing Editor: Clare Churly
Editor: Jo Wilson
Art Director: Jonathan Christie
Senior Art Editor: Juliette Norsworthy
UK editors: Nicole Foster, Alison Bolus, Alex Stetter
Production Manager: Peter Hunt

DEDICATION

Ellen:

Thanks so much to my wonderful husband, David, and my two amazing sons, Winston and Branch. You guys are the best, and I can't wait to take you out for a big carb-filled Italian dinner!

Frances:

A special thank you to my sweet husband, Jon, and daughter, Willa, for their patience and support and for trying all those carbo-licious recipes.

CONTENTS

ACKNOWLEDGEMENTS

I'VE BEEN ON SOME TYPE OF DIET since I was 15 years old. Using a bit of (scary!) addition, that means for the past 36 years I've been counting calories, fasting, juicing, chewing gum, avoiding carbs, avoiding fat, avoiding sugar, and generally obsessing about my weight.

I know I'm not alone here: Weight control is something that *Health* magazine's and Health.com's 14 million readers obsess about, too. So we decided to dedicate ourselves to finding a way out of all this diet madness – and uncover a whole new way to eat. It has always been our dream to create a plan that would allow each and every one of us to relax and enjoy eating again.

I'm a *CarbLover* from way back … and I was *soooo* tired of feeling guilty about every slice of bread and each ounce of pasta I ate. That's why I was excited when two years ago, *Health's* amazing Food Editor, Frances Largeman-Roth, RD, and our in-house weight-loss guru, associate editor Shaun Chavis, told me the news about Resistant Starch, a type of carbohydrate researchers were really talking about: All their studies were showing that Resistant Starch could boost metabolism; curb cravings, lower cholesterol … it looked like this miracle carb could be the solution to our eternal diet problems. *Health's* editors followed the studies, and talked to the experts, and it soon became clear that the era of low-carb eating might soon be OVER! A new and better way of eating was about to dawn.

Here it is … in your hands, the product of voluminous and careful research and rigorous testing by everyone here at *Health*. As our one (and only!) weight-loss book, it was important to us that you be as thrilled with our diet plan as we are. This is truly a diet you can stick with – and enjoy – for the rest of your life.

Of course, many people helped create this groundbreaking plan:

First, a huge thank you to the whole *Health* staff, who worked so tirelessly on *CarbLover's*, all while putting out a great magazine and website: Shaun Chavis and Jennifer Slaton – you guys are simply amazing. And Amy O'Connor, editor in chief of Health.com:

There would be no *CarbLover's* without your initiative and incredibly hard work! Also making it happen from *Health*: Dave Watt, Renee Tulenko, Ben Margherita, Lisa Lombardi, Su Reid-St. John (thanks for that amazing workout!), Marybeth Welsh Dulany, Faustina Williams, Jen Furmaniak, Susan Hall, Rozalynn Frazier, Kimberly Holland, Michael Gollust, our incomparable medical editor Roshini Rajapaksa, MD, and Health. com's Mara Betsch, who, with Amy O'Connor, helped coordinate the fabulous online version of *CarbLover's*.

A huge thanks to Sylvia Auton and John L. Brown for being such wonderful supporters of *Health* and giving us all the tools we needed to create this book. Thanks, too, to the terrific editors of Time Home Entertainment Inc. and Oxmoor House: Richard Fraiman, Jim Childs, Susan Payne Dobbs, Sydney Webber, Tom Mifsud, Fonda Hitchcock and Laurie Herr. Another round of thanks to our crack legal team: Rebecca Sanhueza, Michelle McHugh and Helen Wan.

There are a number of other people who did incredible work helping us get this book to you: They include reporter/researcher Alisa Bowman; dietitians Dawn Jackson Blatner, RD, and Marissa Lippert, RD; and recipe developer extraordinaire Shea Zukowski. A special thank you to Maxine Davidowitz for her brilliant *CarbLover's* design; to Scott Mowbray for helping us get going on the project; to José Perez for helping focus our efforts; and to Debra Richman, Heidi Krupp, and their teams, for helping us spread the word so quickly and so well about the magic of *CarbLover's*.

Frances wants to give a huge thank you to Rhonda Witwer at National Starch and Hope Warshaw, RD, for sharing their Resistant Starch knowledge. And a special thanks, too, from Frances to *Health*'s Leslie Barrie and Caylin Harris for "helping me keep my head on straight!"

And our deepest gratitude goes to those who lost big on *The CarbLover's Diet* and helped us fine-tune the diet so millions of you could experience the thrill of getting slim WHILE eating carbs. We couldn't have done it without you!

Ellen Kunes,
Editor in Chief, *Health* magazine

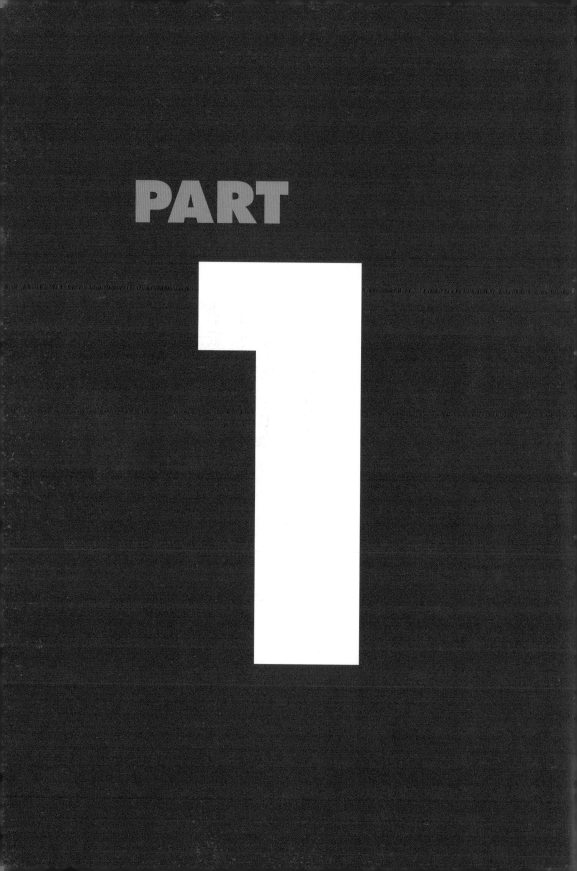

PART

1

Eat Carbs, Get Thin

Chapter 1

You Can Get and Stay Slim on Carbs ... Really!

NOT SO LONG AGO, I was at one of my book club's potluck dinners: We'd been reading the best-selling memoir *Eat, Pray, Love*, so I brought an amazingly tasty pesto pasta salad to mark the fabulous Italian "Eat" section so lovingly detailed in the book. Then I watched as my six friends each took a tiny spoonful of my pasta dish – treating it as if it was a nugget of plutonium on plates that they'd otherwise dutifully filled with sliced chicken breast (no gravy, of course!) and salad (dressing on the side, naturally!). After they had devoured their morsels of pasta, they practically licked the spot on the plate where it had been. Then they proceeded to talk about how guilty they felt for eating a forkful of carbs!

Carbo-phobia!

This "fear of carbs" is rampant: Almost every woman I know has it. We've learned to fear carbs because we've been told for more than 25 years that foods filled with carbohydrates make us gain weight. If you're like me, that means that you're afraid of eating toast with your eggs in the morning. You're afraid of a simple cheese sandwich. You're afraid of baked potatoes. You're afraid of pizza. You're afraid of pasta. Every time you eat one of these delicious basics of a happy, pleasure-filled life, you're overcome with guilt – and the conviction that you are now going to pile on the pounds. Fast.

Well, we, the editors of *Health* magazine, have big news for you. Trust me when I say that if you're carbo-phobic, it has to end right here, right now.

That's because there is new research – reliable, solid, groundbreaking research by the cleverest minds in nutrition science right now – that reveals our old, beloved, carb-filled foods will NOT make us fat. Instead, they will actually make us THIN.

You Can Lose Weight on Carbs!

You're probably wondering – so what's changed? Maybe you're feeling cheated once again by the diet experts. So let me tell you how we first learned about the new "carb-think" and why it inspired us not only to write about it in *Health* magazine, but also to create our very first weight-loss book.

Two years ago, one of my editors mentioned some new research on carbohydrates that she had heard at a scientific conference in Philadelphia. The nutrition experts there seemed very excited about it, she said. "Would you take a look at the research?"

So I did – and what I read reversed a lifetime of assumptions I had about what makes people lose weight and keep it off.

The most astonishing studies were conducted by scientists at The University of Colorado Health Sciences Center for Human Nutrition, in Denver, along with a team of international researchers.[1] They uncovered new evidence that revealed eating the right carbs is the best way to get *and* stay slim.[2] These exciting new studies showed that certain carb-rich foods act as metabolism boosters and appetite suppressants in your body. I'll lay out all the important details of what the researchers uncovered in Chapter 2, but the bottom line

"I watched as my six friends
each took a tiny spoonful of
my pasta dish – treating it as if
it was a nugget of plutonium."

is that rather than making you fat and bloated, carbs can actually do this:

- shrink fat cells, especially in your stomach
- boost fat burning
- preserve muscle mass
- curb cravings
- keep you feeling full longer than other foods
- control blood sugar
- lower cholesterol and triglycerides

Around the same time, other research centres (including those at The University of South Carolina, The University of Minnesota, Louisiana State University and even prestigious centres in Australia, Great Britain and Denmark) were coming to similar conclusions.[3, 4]

Perhaps the most surprising piece of research was a large-scale look into the eating patterns that determine whether people will be fat or skinny over the course of a lifetime. **This multicentre study of 4,451 people found something stunning: It concluded that the slimmest people ate the most carbs (in the form of wholegrains, fruits and vegetables), and the chubbiest people ate the fewest carbs.**[5] The researchers even found that your odds of getting and staying slim are best when carbs comprise up to 64 per cent of your total calorie intake, or 361 grams a day. That's the equivalent of several baked potatoes (a food you've probably avoided for decades).

None of the low-carb diets I've ever tried allowed me to eat that many carbs. Most of the diets I've tried in the past 25 years have limited the carb count to less than 30 per cent of total calories allowed. A few even kept the total to just 10 per cent of total calories.

All of this means that if you're a long-time low-carb dieter and you eat double or even triple the amount of carbs you've been allowing yourself – you won't get fat. In fact, you'll finally be eating the way the slimmest people have been eating all along!

Getting Ready To Lose Weight on Carbs

If you've been convinced for years that eating carbs will make you fat, it's going to take time for you to adjust to the new reality that they are the best things that ever happened to your waistline.

There's something else I have to tell you right now before we begin. And that is, although this is a diet plan that will show you how to live a life full of wonderful, soul-satisfying carbs, being a *CarbLover* does not mean you get to stuff yourself with cakes and biscuits all day. What you'll be doing on this plan is increasing your total intake of carbs and upping the percentage of a type of carb called "Resistant Starch" in your diet. Resistant Starch is a kind of carbohydrate getting lots of attention in scientific circles these days. Yes, it has a strange name, but it's called that for a very good, and very important, reason: It resists digestion.

This is a great boon for weight loss (and your overall health) because Resistant Starch doesn't get absorbed into the bloodstream in the small intestine like other foods – but it does create a chain reaction in your body, literally shrinking fat cells, preserving muscle, stoking your metabolism, and making you feel fuller, longer.

Ask the carb pro

Frances Largeman-Roth, RD

Q. What's the best way to get ready to start *The CarbLover's Diet*?

A. You want to start this new diet feeling energetic and clear-headed. So instead of a last-ditch binge, hold a kitchen reorganization party. Gather all of your Power Pantry items (page 41). Store your grains, and mark your containers. Plan your recipes for the week, and prep some of what you'll be eating the following day. And get a good night's sleep!

Studies show that adding a little Resistant Starch to your to morning meal will shift your body into fat-melting mode so that you burn nearly 25 per cent more calories a day. Meanwhile, you'll eat about 10 per cent fewer calories – simply because you're not as hungry (foods containing Resistant Starch are quite filling, so you end up eating less overall).[6]

But here's the best news of all: Resistant Starch-filled foods aren't those exotic, super-expensive ingredients you can only get via mail-order from Hawaii. They're right here, at your local supermarket. They are bread, cereals, potatoes (even potato crisps!) and bananas (we'll give you a more detailed list on pages 32–33). In other words, the foods with the highest Resistant Starch levels just happen to be delicious, affordable and satisfying – and you can find them at any grocery store. These are the real foods you've been hungry for – and don't ever have to be deprived of again.

Lose Fast on The 7-Day *CarbLover's* Kickstart Plan

The *CarbLover's* Diet begins with a 7-Day *CarbLover's* Kickstart Plan (starting on page 59) developed by two top dietitians. We know how hard it may be to allow yourself, after years of denying yourself delicious carbs, to start eating them again. That's why our 7-Day *CarbLover's* Kickstart Plan helps the transition to your new world of eating and feeling satisfied. On it, you'll quickly knock off up to 2.5 kg (6 lb) and reduce bloating, all the while feeling full, in control and super-energized!

Drop More on The 21-Day *CarbLover's* Immersion Plan

After you've tasted success on the 7-Day *CarbLover's* Kickstart Plan, you're ready for the life-changing 21-Day *CarbLover's* Immersion Plan (starting on page 72). This is the heart and soul of The *CarbLover's* Diet. It's basically a plan that gets you back to the way you used to eat before you made carb deprivation a way of life. The Plan itself is a breeze. Our experts have done all the calculations for you, so all you have to do is eat and enjoy.

Think of the 21-Day *CarbLover's* Immersion Plan as a road-map to the future – an incredibly easy-to-follow set of basic eating rules, daily menus, grab-and-go foods, and delicious recipes anyone can make, enjoy and share with others. Don't feel like cooking? No problem. We've got more than 100 quick bites that work with The *CarbLover's* Diet, too.

Together, we'll wade into virgin territory, which will soon find you: shopping for new ingredients (or yummy grab-and-go items) at the supermarket; cooking up simple, delicious recipes; ordering what you want at your favourite restaurants; and enjoying meals with friends and family – all while getting and staying slim. We'll support your new eating life with tips, recipes and clear-cut meal plans that will change your relationship with food and keep you from ever going hungry again. By the end of this three weeks, you'll have lost up to another 2.5 kg (6 lb)!

Becoming a *CarbLover* for Life

In Chapter 8, you'll find proven get-to-goal strategies, including ideas for helping you reach your goal weight even faster if you make some small tweaks to your lifestyle. Exercise, smarter sleep habits and cooking tricks can speed up weight loss while you're still enjoying carbs.

As you lose weight, our dietitians – as well as real women who've already successfully lost weight on *CarbLover's* – will encourage you every step of the way. If you have a little "I can't believe I ate that muffin!" panic attack, we're there too ... with real-life advice from women who've lost big, as well as experts who can reassure you that the road map to lasting weight loss is the very one you are on. Finally, when you've reached your goal weight, we'll tell you how to stay as slim as you want to be, forever (starting on page 251).

So get ready for the best – and only – diet plan you'll ever need. Do you love making special meals for friends and family? Have we got some great recipes for you! You can also have a great social life while on *CarbLover's:* Enjoy a glass of wine (and some amazing pasta salad!) with your book group! Or how about tacos (pages 104 and 172) after work with colleagues? You can create decadent desserts your family will love, like our *CarbLover's* Dark Chocolate & Oat Clusters (page 213). In fact, in Chapter 7, you'll find over 75 easy, tasty recipes for nearly every eating moment of your life.

We've also built an easy-to-navigate website. At **carblovers.com,** you'll find even more recipes, meet other dieters, and get real-time advice from the same experts who helped create this groundbreaking plan. Turn the page, and start eating what you love, and at the very same time, start dropping that stubborn 5, 10, 40 kg (12, 25, 100 lb) or more! Get ready to feel satisfied, happy and oh-so-slim. Get ready for your fabulous new life as a *CarbLover*!

"I Lost Weight on *CarbLover's*"

BEFORE

ALI HOCART

Age: 39
Height: 1.6 m (5' 3")
**Weight before: 74.4 kg
(11 st 10 lb)**
**Weight after: 63.5 kg
(10 st)**
**Weight lost: 10.9 kg
(24 lb)**

Biggest success moment:
I've gone from someone people
called "pretty but chunky" to "the
incredible shrinking woman". It feels
great!
Biggest challenge: On my
previous diet attempts, I failed in
silence. This time, I asked for support
and encouragement – and got it.
Favourite recipe: I'm a real bread-
and-cheese person, so my favourites
were the Cheddar & Egg on Rye
(page 134) and the Tomato &
Mozzarella Melt (page 136).

AFTER

I struggled to lose weight for years. Even though I was a serial dieter, somehow I could never stay slim. I tried diets with packaged foods and meals, like Jenny Craig and The Zone, as well as high-protein plans. Inevitably I'd get discouraged, quit, regain the weight – and sometimes I'd put on even more! I was so frustrated that I committed to a serious exercise routine. But even after months of working out with a trainer, it became clear that exercise alone wasn't going to be enough. That was a difficult reality to face. *CarbLover's* was my last chance, so I decided to give it a try. The first thing I did was give up diet drinks and prepared diet-food junk. Then I started cooking from scratch and taking my lunch to work instead of eating out. For the first time in forever I was eating whole, real food – and feeling my taste buds come alive again!

I like how *CarbLover's* lets you eat what you want, but teaches you to manage your cravings. For example, I love rich chocolate cakes and pastries. So I made up something that reminds me of a chocolate croissant: I sprinkle a tablespoon of dark chocolate chips on a corn tortilla (Resistant Starch!), put it under the grill for 45 seconds, and roll it up. It's amazing!

After just 12 weeks on *CarbLover's*, I'm halfway to my goal. People tell me my skin looks better. My confidence has improved dramatically. I'm so excited about getting dressed in the morning and being able to shop for clothes again.

Chapter 2

The Truth About Low-Carb Diets

(and Why You Gotta Eat Carbs to Be Slim)

FINALLY, THE TRUTH COMES OUT: Those low-carb diets (all of them!) you've been trying to follow for the last 1, 7, even 10, years? According to experts, in the long run, low-carb diets just don't work! Now, it's true that low-carbohydrate, high-protein plans can help you lose weight in the short term. Over the past 10 years, I've lost 20 pounds ... and then gained that same 20 pounds back – maybe five times! – on a variety of low-carb plans. My experience, say diet researchers, is all too common. In fact, nutrition researchers say that limiting your carbs just doesn't work over the long haul because we are hardwired to crave carbohydrates.

And that spells carb-fuelled BINGES. With all those binges, it is absolutely inevitable that you'll gain back most, if not all, of the weight you lost on that low-carb diet in the first place. Want to know a few more reasons why you need to steer clear of the low-carb way of life? Read on.

5 TRUTHS ABOUT LOW-CARB DIETS

1. Low-carb diets make you feel sad and stressed!

Snapping at your husband and kids? Yelling at the driver in front of you who just isn't going fast enough? You might want to blame your carb-deprivation. A recent study by Australian researchers, published in the *Archives of Internal Medicine*, followed 106 dieters for a year. Half ate a carb-rich diet; the others followed a low-carb diet. After a year, the carb-eaters felt happier, calmer and more focused than the carb-deprived group, who reported feeling stressed out. [1] Another study at The University of Toronto found that dieters who restricted carbs for just three days reported feeling more depressed than before restricting them. [2] The reason? Carbs boost mood-regulating, stress-reducing chemicals in the brain, and high-protein, fatty foods may deplete them, says Grant Brinkworth, PhD, lead researcher of the Australian study.

2. Low-carb diets make you fatter, not thinner!

The stress and depression low-carb dieters feel eventually derails their best efforts to stay slim. That's because stress produces high levels of hormones, like cortisol, which boost your appetite and can lead to bingeing, says obesity researcher Elissa Epel, PhD, associate professor in the Department of Psychiatry at The University of California, San Francisco.

3. Low-carb diets are not sustainable!

It's one thing to tough out a low-carb diet for six weeks or even six months. It's another to do it for a lifetime, and studies show that people have a harder time sticking with low-carb rather than high-carb diets. In a 2009 Israeli study of 322 dieters, only 78 per cent of those on low-carb plans stuck with their diets for the long term (up to two years), while nearly 90 per cent of those who ate a more balanced-in-carbs diet were still going strong after two years.[3] "It's hard to consistently follow a diet that is very low in carbs or very high in carbs," says weight-loss researcher Anwar T. Merchant, ScD, DMD, associate professor of epidemiology and biostatistics at The University of South Carolina.

"Carbs boost mood-regulating, stress-reducing chemicals in the brain."

4. Low-carb diets bloat your stomach!

Think carbs are the reason you can't do up your trousers? Think again. According to the National Institute of Digestive Diseases, bloating is one of the key symptoms of constipation. And constipation is a common side effect of a low-carb diet. In one study, as many as 68 per cent of participants on a low-carb diet complained of constipation.[4] That's compared to just 30 per cent of the general non-dieting population and 35 per cent of dieters who ate more carbs.

5. Low-carb diets make you feel deprived!

Any dieter who has managed to stick to a very low-carb diet for any length of time knows that they start craving carbs. And it's not your imagination. According to research at The University of Toronto, carb deprivation leads directly to carb bingeing. In one study of 89 women, half restricted the amount of carbs they ate, while the other half did not. After three days, when both groups were served a breakfast and told to eat all that they wanted, the women on the low-carb diet stuffed themselves with calorie and fat-laden carbs (like croissants), while the women who had been on diets with a balanced amount of carbs continued to follow their diets.[5] Bottom line: If you stop eating carbs, it's almost impossible not to binge on them when given the opportunity.

The Amazing News About Carb-Rich Diets

While there is now solid research that reveals low-carb diets are destined to fail, there is just as much evidence – in fact, even more evidence – that eating a diet packed with the right kind of carbs is *the secret to getting and staying slim for life*

When we talk about the right kind of carb, what we mean is the kind of carbohydrate called Resistant Starch. Nearly 200 important studies conducted at respected universities and research centres around the world have shown Resistant Starch to be an extraordinary, 100-per cent natural appetite suppressant and metabolism booster that will change the way you think about dieting forever.

Resistant Starch is a carbohydrate that *resists digestion*. It's found in ordinary foods you already eat and can buy at any supermarket. All of this solid research shows that consuming more of this special carbohydrate helps you:

- eat less
- burn more calories
- feel more energized and less stressed
- steady blood sugar levels

The science behind Resistant Starch is truly incredible: We explain exactly how it works later in this chapter.

But first, because we know you've been conditioned for so long to think of bread and pasta and rice and potatoes as bad-for-you foods, we want to explain to you all the reasons why getting carbs back into your diet isn't only good for you ... it's absolutely essential if you want to lose weight and keep it off for the rest of your life.

The top weight-loss experts we've talked to all agree. "There are three things that dictate success with losing weight and maintaining that weight loss," says veteran weight-loss researcher Larry Tucker, PhD, a professor of exercise science at Brigham Young University in Provo, Utah: "The diet has to be healthy, it has to be effective, and it has to be sustainable. It can't be something that you think you can tough out for a few weeks or a few months. It has to be something that eventually becomes a lifestyle." And that lifestyle, explains diet researcher Dr Merchant, *must* include a healthy helping of foods like bread, potatoes, fruits and vegetables. "The good news is that people who maintain an optimal body weight are not following a very low-carbohydrate diet or a very high-carbohydrate diet," he says. "They are eating regular, balanced meals that include carbs."

There's barely enough room in this book to list the solid, evidence-based reasons you must get carbs back in your life if you are ever to achieve the sleek, slim look you've been wanting for so long. Here are a few, though, that we thought you should absolutely commit to memory.

9 REASONS YOU NEED CARBS IN YOUR LIFE

1. Eating carbs makes you thin for life!

As I mentioned in Chapter 1, a recent multicentre study of thousands of people found that the slimmest people also ate the most carbs, and the chubbiest ate the least. The researchers concluded that your odds of getting and staying slim are best when carbs comprise up to 64 per cent of your total calorie intake, or 361 grams a day. That's the equivalent of several baked potatoes (a food we bet you've been afraid to eat for decades).[6] None of the low-carb diets I've ever tried allowed you to eat that many carbs. In fact, most low-carb diets limit you to fewer than 30 per cent of total calories, or 150 grams a day. And some low-carb diets have almost no carbs at all: They have as little as 10 per cent of calories from carbs!

The CarbLover's Diet allows you to double, even triple your carb intake – compared to low-carb plans – so you can start eating the way the slimmest people have been eating all along.

2. Carbs fill you up!

Many carb-filled foods act as powerful appetite suppressants. They're even more filling than protein or fat. These special carbs fill you up because they are digested more slowly than other types of foods. The carbs in *The CarbLover's Diet* quickly trigger a sensation of fullness in both your brain and your stomach. As a result, you stay satisfied longer – so much longer that you'll find that you eat less automatically. Research done at The University of Surrey in Great Britain found that consuming Resistant Starch in one meal caused study participants to consume 10 per cent fewer calories (roughly 150 to 200 calories for the average woman) during the next day because they felt less hungry.[7]

3. Carbs curb your hunger!

These good-news carbs also raise levels of satiety hormones that tell the brain to flip a switch that stifles hunger and turns up metabolism. "High-fibre carbohydrates such as brown rice and grains allow you to eat to the point of satisfaction and still lose weight " says Tucker. "You can lose weight, and you don't have to be hungry at all."

4. Carbs control blood sugar and help prevent diabetes!

The right mix of carbs is the best way to control blood sugar and thus keep type 2 diabetes at bay. In one study done at the Beltsville Human Nutrition Research Center at the United States Department of Agriculture, participants who consumed a diet rich in the foods featured in *The CarbLover's Diet* were able to lower their post-meal blood sugar and insulin response by up to 38 per cent.[8] *The CarbLover's Diet* lets you eat all the carbs you want, but we've combined them with other foods so that they don't cause a spike in your blood sugar. Instead, you'll be enjoying carbs that keep your blood sugar more balanced than traditional low-carb diets.

5. Carbs speed up metabolism!

The CarbLover's Diet is filled with carbohydrates that speed up your metabolism and your body's other natural fat-burners. As Resistant Starch moves through your digestive system, it releases fatty acids that encourage fat burning, especially around your waist. [9]

6. Carbs protect muscle while burning fat!

The right carbs produce a fatty acid that helps you preserve muscle mass – and that stokes your metabolism, thus helping you lose weight faster. When researchers set out to fatten up a bunch of mice, they fed one group of rodents food that was low in Resistant Starch and a second group Resistant Starch-packed food. The mice who were fed the chow that was low in Resistant Starch got fat and flabby – gaining fat and losing muscle mass. Mice that ate the meals high in Resistant Starch preserved their muscle mass, keeping their metabolisms humming along.[10]

7. Carbs blast belly fat!

Carbs help you lose your stomach fat faster than other foods, even when the same number of calories are consumed. When scientists fed mice a diet rich in Resistant Starch, it increased the activity of fat-burning enzymes and decreased the activity of fat-storage enzymes. This means that the stomach-fat cells were less likely to pick up and store calories as fat.[11]

8. Carbs keep you satisfied!

Carbs keep you satisfied longer than other foods. Here's why: Your brain acts like a computerized fuel gauge that directs you to fill up whenever it notices that its petrol tank (your stomach) is empty. It gets these messages from nerves that surround the stomach. It receives messages from various hormones, too. These hormones come from your stomach, your intestines, your pancreas and your fat cells. Some hormones communicate "empty". Others communicate "full". When many "empty" messages come in at once, the brain turns up those "I'm hungry" signals *and* turns down metabolism. Conversely, when "I'm full" messages come in, appetite decreases and metabolism gets ramped up to fat-burning mode.

Your appetite on carbs

CarbLover's carbs curb hunger better than other types of foods for two reasons. For one thing, they're rich in super-satisfying fibre and Resistant Starch – plus *CarbLover's* carbs are low in calories but high in volume, meaning you get toput way more on your plate. Proof: 500 g (1 lb) boiled, diced potatoes have nearly the same amount of calories as 125 g (4 oz) grated Cheddar cheese.

THE *CARBLOVER'S* PROMISE AT A GLANCE

Want to know how eating carbohydrates fills you up on fewer calories, stokes your metabolism, steadies your blood sugar and lets you eat what you want when you want it? Check out this head-to-toe chart.

Brain You'll be eating foods that help fullness hormones like leptin do their job, turning off appetite and turning up your metabolic furnace.

Mouth CarbLover's recipes are high in flavour, but low in calories. They will delight and satisfy your taste buds, allowing you to feel full sooner during a meal.

Stomach Most of the food on this plan is heavy – in a good way. It will weigh down your stomach so you feel full.

Fat cells The Resistant Starch on this plan will trigger fat cells to release their contents so muscle and other cells can burn it for energy.

Bloodstream CarbLover's is rich in foods that keep blood sugar levels steady, so you never experience those sudden drops in energy that lead to a stand-in-front-of-the-fridge binge.

Eyes You'll eat frequently on this plan – roughly every few hours. You will also have the opportunity to eat a wide variety of your favourite foods. So no matter how tempting those doughnuts are at coffee time, you'll be able to tell yourself, "I can eat something just as satisfying very soon I don't need that right now."

Liver Because Carb-Lover's shifts your body into a fat-burning state, your liver will hold on to its stores of glycogen and water. That way, most of the weight you lose early on in this plan will come from fat and not from water.

Gut The high fibre content of the CarbLover's plan means that food moves more slowly through your digestive system, causing slow and even rises in blood sugar levels. The Resistant Starch releases fatty acids that turn down appetite, keep blood sugar steady and turn up fat burning.

Muscles On other diets, you lose muscle. On CarbLover's, you'll preserve it, so your metabolism remains stoked.

CarbLover's feeds your body with ultra-satisfying foods – foods that flip on every single fullness trigger in your body. They release fullness hormones in the intestine. They make your cells more sensitive to insulin. They help you get over that initial hump in dieting. By increasing your consumption of filling foods and releasing satiety hormones, *CarbLover's* minimizes the hunger and cravings that makes so many dieters call it quits.

9. Carbs make you feel good – about you!

"Dieters feel so empowered once they lose weight on carbs. For the first time, they are able to lose weight by eating in a balanced manner, without cutting out entire food groups," says Sari Greaves, RD, spokesperson for the American Dietetic Association.

RESISTANT STARCH: THE ULTIMATE FAT-BURNING CARB

You've probably figured out that *The CarbLover's Diet* is going to sneak Resistant Starch into your diet, and you're right! But what the heck is it? Where do you get it? Is it going to bust your budget? And what does it taste like? Relax. Lots of foods you already have in your store cupboard are loaded with Resistant Starch (see Top Resistant Starch Foods, page 32). And you don't need a lot of Resistant Starch to get dramatic weight-loss results.

Carbohydrate-rich foods (like your old friends bread, potatoes, grains and fruit) actually contain two types of starch. One is high-glycaemic starch. Like sugar, it's absorbed into the bloodstream quickly, raising blood sugar. This also causes a spike in energy. Another is called Resistant Starch, so named because it *resists digestion*. Resistant Starch is neither new nor experimental. As we mentioned earlier, nearly 200 studies have been conducted on Resistant Starch. Most of them are large, multicentre studies published in peer-reviewed medical journals like the *Archives of Internal Medicine*.

These studies show that Resistant Starch is a weight-loss powerhouse because it does not get absorbed into the bloodstream or broken down into glucose. Therefore, it does not raise blood sugar. It travels through your digestive system nearly intact. That's where Resistant Starch triggers the incredible benefits mentioned earlier. It produces fatty acids that promote weight loss by:

- Turning on enzymes that melt fat, especially in the abdominal area.
- Encouraging your liver to switch to a fat-burning state.
- Boosting satiety hormones that make you get and stay full longer. [12]

How Much Resistant Starch Is Enough?

Most people consume only about 4.8 grams of Resistant Starch a day, but researchers believe we need more for optimal health and weight loss.[13] That's why the *CarbLover's* menus include 10 to 15 grams daily of this important fat-burning nutrient, served up in delicious recipes like Chicken Pasta Primavera (page 107) and Coconut French Toast with Raspberry Syrup (page 126).

Resistant Starch is definitely the star on *The CarbLover's Diet,* but it's got a strong supporting cast of foods. This plan doesn't take one "exotic" food and build an entire diet around it – ignoring the fact that you can't live on one food or one food group for the rest of your life. This is about losing weight and keeping it off forever. You'll only be able to do that if all the foods you love are on the menu. Turn to pages 32–33 for a preview of what you'll be eating on *CarbLover's.*

Ask the carb pro

Frances Largeman-Roth, RD

Q. **How can I be sure I'm getting enough Resistant Starch?**

A. **Here's a quick solution: Eat one slightly green banana a day,** either in your Banana Shake (page 99) or as a snack. That will guarantee you 12.5 grams of Resistant Starch so you can achieve your weight loss goals without feeling hungry.

"Resistant Starch might sound exotic – but the foods that have it are probably in your kitchen right now! As a bonus, they're affordable, tasty and easy to prepare."

TOP RESISTANT STARCH FOODS

FOOD	Serving Size	Grams of Resistant Starch per Serving
BANANA, green	1 medium 18–20 cm/7–8"	12.5
BANANA, ripe	1 medium 18–20 cm/7–8"	4.7
OATS, uncooked/toasted	50 g (2 oz)	4.6
BEANS, cannellini, cooked/canned	125 g (4 oz)	3.8
LENTILS, cooked	100 g (3½ oz)	3.4
POTATOES, cooked and cooled	1 potato, small	3.2
PLANTAIN, cooked	75 g (3 oz)	2.7
CHICKPEAS, cooked/canned	125 g (4 oz) cup	2.1
PASTA, wholewheat, cooked	150 g (5 oz)	2.0
BARLEY, pearl, cooked	75 g (3 oz)	1.9
PASTA, white, cooked and cooled	150 g (5 oz)	1.9
BEANS, kidney, cooked/canned	125 g (4 oz)	1.8
POTATOES, boiled (skin & flesh)	1 potato, small	1.8
RICE, brown, cooked	100 g (3½ oz)	1.7
BEANS, pinto, cooked/canned	125 g (4 oz)	1.6
PEAS, canned/frozen	75 g (3 oz)	1.6
PASTA, white, cooked	150 g (5 oz)	1.5
BEANS, black cooked/canned	125 g (4 oz)	1.5

FOOD	Serving Size	Grams of Resistant Starch per Serving
MILLET, cooked	75 g (3 oz)	1.5
POTATOES, baked (skin & flesh)	1 small	1.4
BREAD, pumpernickel	25 g (1 oz) slice	1.3
POLENTA, cooked	8 tablespoons	1.0
YAM, cooked	100 g (3½ oz) cubes	1.0
POTATO CRISPS	25 g (1 oz)	1.0
CORNFLAKES	25 g (1 oz)	0.9
BREAD, RYE (whole)	25 g (1 oz) slice	0.9
PUFFED WHEAT	15 g (½ oz)	0.9
TORTILLAS, corn	25 g (1 oz) tortilla	0.8
ENGLISH MUFFIN	1 whole muffin	0.7
BREAD, sourdough	25 g (1 oz) slice	0.6
CRACKERS, rye	2 crispbreads	0.6
PORRIDGE	240 ml (8 fl oz)	0.5
BREAD, Italian	25 g (1 oz)	0.3
BREAD, wholegrain	25 g (1 oz) slice	0.3
CORN CHIPS	25 g (1 oz)	0.2
CRISPBREADS, Melba toast	4 rounds	0.2

"I Lost Weight on *CarbLover's*"

BEFORE

JOY BUTTS

Age **34**
Height **1.65 m (5' 5")**
Weight before **65.8 kg (10 st 5 lb)**
Weight after **61.7 kg (9 st 10 lb)**
Weight lost **4.1 kg (9 lb)**

Biggest success moment: My out-of-town boyfriend, whom I see every two weeks, jokes that I get smaller every time he sees me.
Biggest challenge: Because of my job, I'm forced to eat out more than most diets allow, so I have to make very conscious choices.
Favourite recipe: Banana Shake (page 99). I can make it before I leave for work, and it kills my sugar cravings.

AFTER

Since I was a teenager, I've tried every diet from Nutrisystem to the Beet Diet. I usually weighed between 59 and 61 kg (about 9 st 7 lb). Five years ago, I joined Weight Watchers and got down to 58 kg (9 st 2 lb). But when I stopped tracking points, the weight came back. **Last year** my workload increased, which meant late nights and eating anything that wasn't nailed down when I got home at 10 p.m. By July, none of my clothes fitted any more, and I weighed 70.3 kg (11 st 1 lb).

I started _CarbLover's_ because I hate low-carb diets; I love to run and need fuel for my workouts! I focused on making one CarbLover's recipe for breakfast, like the Banana Shake (page 99). The Express Lunch Plate (page 103) seemed like a good fit for my lifestyle, but I was sceptical of how little food it contained. When I tried it, I was shocked that I worked through the entire afternoon without feeling hungry.

When I go out to eat, spotting the wholegrains on the menu is easier than I thought. I found a restaurant near my flat that serves lentil soup with wholemeal pitta bread. I steer my friends to burger joints with granary buns or pizza places with wholemeal crust.

I always dreaded running while on a diet, but this diet kicked up my energy levels. I've run two marathons before, but I've never felt as strong as I do now. My legs feel strong, and I breathe easily without huffing and puffing! After just two months on _CarbLover's_, I've lost 4.1 kg (9 lb) and have more stamina than ever.

Chapter 3

The *CarbLover's* Diet Rules

MOST DIETS FEATURE one "star" food or ingredient, and the entire diet is built around it. The trouble is, no one can live on one food or food group without going absolutely nuts! As we mentioned in Chapter 2, while Resistant Starch is definitely the star food in The *CarbLover's* Diet, it has a strong supporting cast. This is a balanced diet, one that includes all the foods you need to look and feel your best. Yes, you'll eat carbs – pasta, bread, potatoes – but you'll also enjoy protein and a little fat, too. And you'll even get wine, chocolate and other treats. We guarantee you won't waste one minute fixating on what you can't eat. Ready for the new rules that will change the way you eat … for life?

5 RULES OF THE *CARBLOVER'S* DIET

1. Eat a CarbStar at every meal.

High-in-Resistant-Starch carbs are the cornerstone of this diet. They are your secret to losing weight without hunger or cravings. Resistant Starch is a miracle ingredient found only in carbohydrate foods. *The CarbLover's Diet* maximizes your intake of this fat-flusher by sneaking the top 11 Resistant Starch foods into every meal. We call these Resistant Starch-rich foods **CarbStars!** Each and every one of them contains at least 1 gram of Resistant Starch per serving. Some, like unripe bananas, contain 12 times that much!

★

BANANAS

★

OATS

★

BEANS AND LENTILS

★

POTATOES

★

WHOLEWHEAT PASTA

★

BARLEY

★

BROWN RICE

★

PEAS

★

RYE AND PUMPERNICKEL BREAD

★

POLENTA

★

POTATO CRISPS

2. Balance your plates.

Depending on where you are in the diet, CarbStars should take up roughly one quarter of your plate. The rest of your meals will be filled with great weight-loss boosters like lean meats and low-fat dairy products, good fats and fruits and veggies (see the list on pages 254–255). For the first few weeks on *The CarbLover's Diet*, stick to the suggested menus, recipes and other food options to make sure you get this balancing act just right. Once you reach your goal, you'll find advice in Chapter 10 for building meals on your own, whether you're at home, at work, at a restaurant … even abroad!

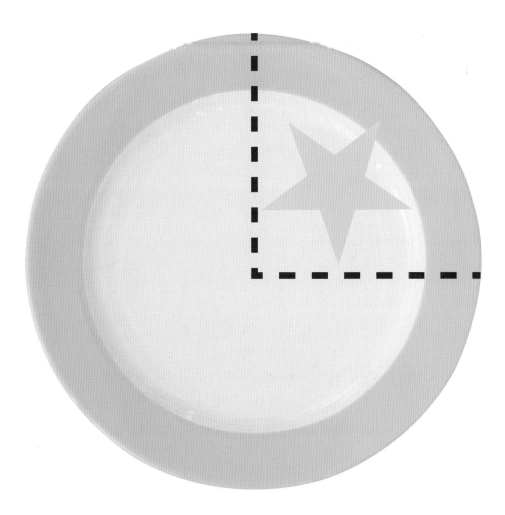

3. Be portion savvy.

Here's the deal on portion control: You can eat the carbs you crave at every meal. That said, you do need to follow our portion advice. The best news, though: We promise you won't feel hungry. You'll discover that the meals on this diet are filling and completely satisfying. (Amazingly, some of our diet testers complained about how often and how much they were eating because they were so used to skipping meals!) The menus and recipes in Chapters 5, 6 and 7 are all carefully calibrated to fill you up – until it's time for your next meal or snack. On page 256, you'll find a handy chart that helps you create your own versions of **CarbLover's** meals and recipes.

4. Never deprive yourself.

Chocolate desserts, pastas, wine, bread, even potato crisps are on *The CarbLover's Diet* menu. Why? When you're forbidden to eat your favourite foods, you end up bingeing on those same foods – and consequently packing on pounds. There's solid research out there that shows this, and yet we continue to follow diets that tell us mostly what we CAN'T eat. I don't know about you, but if I'm told I can't eat pizza, I crave it more than ever, and then when I do break down and have some, I eat about five slices ... not just one. On *Carblover's*, you won't have to give up the one food or beverage that you really love. You can indulge (in moderation) every day.

Your looks on carbs

Switch from a low-carb diet to one that's rich in wholegrains, fruits and veggies, and your skin will start to glow within weeks, says Doris Day, MD, clinical assistant professor of dermatology at New York University. Fruit – especially berries – is a serious beauty booster. It's packed with vitamin C and antioxidants; both improve your skin's elasticity and smooth wrinkles.

5. Build a power pantry.

To succeed with our plan, it's vital that you have a store cupboard stocked with our CarbStars and other important foods – so you're not tempted to go off the diet. Some of the same fat-burning foods are featured over and over again on this diet. Make sure you have the following within reach at all times:

In Your Store Cupboard

Almonds, walnuts, other nuts and seeds (unsalted)
Almond and peanut butter (natural)
Baked potato crisps
Barley
Brown rice
Canned beans
Coconut, dessicated
Cornflakes
Croutons
Dates
Low-fat balsamic vinaigrette
Oats (preferably rolled or pinhead)
Olive oil
Polenta
Quinoa
Rye crackers
Tortilla chips
Vinegar
Wholemeal bread
Wholemeal pasta

In Your Refrigerator

Berries
Broccoli
Carrots
Semi-skimmed or 1% fat milk
Low-fat cheese
Olives
Pears
Potatoes and sweet potatoes
Salmon
Tortillas
Yogurt, preferably low-fat Greek

In Your Freezer

Frozen fruit
Frozen veg

On Your Worktop

Apples
Avocados
Bananas
Pears
Tomatoes

The CarbLover's Diet includes staples from EVERY food group!

WHAT'S ON THE *CARBLOVER'S* MENU?

Potatoes!

Baked potatoes, sweet potatoes, yams and even potato crisps are on the menu. In addition to **fibre** and **Resistant Starch,** potatoes are a natural source of a proteinase inhibitor, a type of protein which appears to increase levels of satiety hormones and reduce appetite.[1] Potatoes of every stripe are also incredibly filling. One large baked potato, for instance, will run you fewer than 300 calories. Even potato crisps are weight-loss friendly, with one serving providing 1 gram of Resistant Starch. They also satisfy your need for crunch, while at the same time providing you with some fibre. If you're going to have a snack crisp, then potato crisps (preferably baked) are the ones you should reach for.

Beans!

These are true stars of the carb world. Not only are they rich in Resistant Starch, but beans and legumes are also your weight-loss secret weapons because they're one of the few foods that packs both types of fibre – soluble and insoluble. *The CarbLover's Diet* makes sure you get the recommended 25 to 35 grams of fibre every day (see the top fibre-filled foods, page 265). Soluble fiber helps you feel full by absorbing water, and it prevents some of the calories you take in from getting absorbed into your bloodstream. It also slows the absorption of glucose, helping keep your blood sugar levels stable. Insoluble fibre is bulky and fills you up, triggering the feeling of satiety. It also keeps things moving, which prevents bloating. A Brigham Young University study of 252 women found that every 1 gram increase in the amount of fibre consumed correlated with 250 g (8 oz) weight loss.[2]

Fruit!

You might have craved other sweets during your last low-carb diet. But lack of fruit probably derailed your weight-loss progress. When Israeli researchers put 322 people on either a low-carb diet, low-fat diet or a Mediterranean diet, dieters rated fruit – not pasta, not biscuits – at the top of their list of longings.[3] "All dieter groups noted fruits as an irresistible food," says Ilana Greenberg, RD, MPH, one of the study's authors. In other words, you can't live without it – and, frankly, there's no reason to try! Certain types of fruit, especially bananas, are rich in Resistant Starch. And other types of fruit are a great source of pectin, a type of soluble fibre found in the rinds and skins of fruit that may block fat storage. In addition to that, fruit is "high volume," and filled with water. This low-calorie density makes it nearly impossible to eat too much fruit. "Fruits and non-starchy vegetables allow you to eat to the point of satisfaction and still lose weight", says Larry Tucker, PhD, a professor at Brigham Young University.

Veggies!

Vegetables such as cucumbers, broccoli and artichokes are a dieter's best friend. They contain almost no calories (100 g (3 oz) raw broccoli has a measly 31 calories!) and are loaded with weight-reducing fiber. So eat up!

Bread, rice, pasta and whole grains!

The CarbLover's Diet is bringing back tortillas, sandwiches, croutons and pasta – especially the wholegrain kinds. These foods satisfy our cravings for crunch and chewiness. More important, they are rich in Resistant Starch and fibre, and research shows that people who consume more wholegrains tend to weigh less and have less body fat than people who skip them.[4]

Fish!

Cold-water fish like salmon and tuna pack a heart-healthy and slimming fatty acid called **omega-3.** Omega-3s speed weight loss by switching on enzymes that trigger fat-burning in cells. They also help boost mood, which may reduce emotional eating. And omega-3s might improve leptin signalling in the brain, making it turn up fat-burning and turn down appetite. A French study of 27 women determined that adding 3 grams daily of fish oil (the amount in roughly 175 g/6 oz) salmon reduced body-fat levels by 3.5 per cent and abdominal fat by 6 per cent.[5] For a list of top omega-3 foods, see page 267.

Nuts and oils!

Most types of nuts and other good-for-you fats, like olive oil, are a rich source of fat-fighting **Monounsaturated Fatty Acids (MUFAs).** One Danish study of 27 men and women found that a diet that included 20 per cent of calories from MUFAs measurably sped up 24-hour calorie- and fat-burning after 6 months.[6] Other research shows that MUFAs are especially good at melting tummy fat.[7] High-MUFA foods – namely peanuts, tree nuts and olive oil – have been shown to keep blood sugar steady and reduce appetite, too. For a list of the top MUFA-rich foods, see page 266.[8]

Meat and dairy!

Steak and macaroni cheese are on the **CarbLover's** menu for a reason: Both contain **Conjugated Linoleic Acid (CLA)**, a fat that is thought to help blood glucose enter body cells so it can be burned for energy and not stored as fat. It's also believed that CLA may help to promote fat burning, especially in muscles, where the bulk of our calorie burning takes place.[9] In an Ohio State University study of 35 women, study participants who took 8 grams of CLA daily lost more weight, especially from fat, compared to women who took a placebo.[10] And a University of Wisconsin study of 23 people who took 4 grams daily of CLA determined that the CLA helped participants burn more fat – even while they were asleep! – than the placebo.[11] Dairy products are also a rich source of calcium, and a University of Tennessee study found that dieters who consumed 1,100 milligrams of calcium daily (upped from 500 milligrams by adding three daily servings of yogurt) lost up to 22 per cent more weight and 61 per cent more body fat than dieters who had consumed significantly less calcium but had eaten the same number of calories.[12] The reason: Calcium is stored in fat cells, and researchers think that the more calcium a fat cell has, the more fat that cell will release to be burned.

Ask the **carb pro**

Frances Largeman-Roth, RD

Q. I'm on a budget. Can I still try *CarbLover's*?

A. You bet! To save even more money, try buying your grains – barley, brown rice and pasta – in bulk. Then store them in airtight containers away from heat and light. This helps them last much longer. Label the container with the name of the grain, the date you purchased it, the correct serving size and cooking instructions. Plan to use it up within 6 months. To store grains for up to a year, keep them in the fridge or freezer.

"I Lost Weight on *CarbLover's*"

BEFORE

RILEY TANT

Age: **23**
Height: **1.72 m (5' 8")**
Weight before: **75.8 kg (11 st 13 lb)**
Weight after: **68.5 kg (10 st 11 lb)**
Pounds lost: **16**

Biggest success moment: Wearing my favourite black-tweed skirt again. Before, it was SO tight that it rode up when I walked (if I was even able to zip it up that day). Now, I have room to tuck my shirt in!

Biggest challenge: Pizza. It's allowed on *CarbLover's*, but I live above a pizzeria, and the smell is tempting!

Favourite recipe: Chicken Pasta Primavera (page 107). I make it in batches and eat it all week!

AFTER

I started CarbLover's for two reasons: I needed a diet that would allow me to cook (even bake!), and I needed to lose the 10-plus pounds I gained during a recent move from Birmingham, Alabama, to New York City. The move was a big adjustment. Take-away food became my new best friend.

CarbLover's taught me to substitute healthier carbs for the junk I was eating. It was easy to swap my breakfast cereal for a banana with almond butter and porridge, but was sceptical of other foods, thinking lentils and quinoa would taste like cardboard. Wrong!

After two weeks on CarbLover's, I got an unexpected benefit: energy! I could work nine hours a day and then hit the gym for a 4-mile run, five times a week, without feeling exhausted afterwards. Even when I started exercising again, I didn't feel hungry on CarbLover's. I actually stopped craving sweets after every meal, and my once-a-day chocolate habit became a once-a-week habit with almost no effort.

Friends came to visit midway through my first month on the diet, and I was worried that I would lose control, but I never did. I chose fruit, yogurt and granola or nuts for breakfast, and then used the portion-control tips on page 39 at lunch and dinner.

I love that CarbLover's isn't too strict. The flexibility, in fact, is why my weight is going down, my waist is shrinking and my energy continues to skyrocket!

Chapter 4

Still Carbo-Phobic? Read This!

BY NOW I HOPE all this news about carbs – and how they're going to help you lose weight for life – has you feeling pretty excited. Even if you've just skimmed the previous chapters, you've still discovered that there's a mountain of research – and real-life success stories! – backing up the CarbLover's promise: You can lose 5, 10, 40-plus kg (12, 25, 100 lb) and keep them off, without feeling hungry.

Still, if you're a veteran dieter, you may be a bit wary. Decades of denying yourself potatoes, pasta, bread, and more has you trained to fear carbs. We understand: Carbo-phobia can't be wiped out overnight! All this talk about eating delicious, formerly-forbidden carbs has alarm bells in your head clanging "fattening! fattening! fattening!"

No worries. We're here to help you get your mind as well as your body ready for CarbLover's. Read on for eight things you must stop worrying about right now!

8 CARB-EATING FEARS TO CONQUER RIGHT NOW

1. Carbs made me heavy in the first place!

The fact is, they didn't. Important research done by big, multicentre studies on thousands of people uncovered this: Slim people eat the most carbs, and the heaviest people eat the least. Still sceptical? Go back to Chapter 2 for details on why carbs did not make you fat – and how *CarbLover's* will make you thin!

2. I'm already eating way too many carbs!

On the contrary, you're probably carb-deficient! The marketers behind fad diets have done a great job convincing people that they are eating too many carbs. In reality, most people eat too few of them – at least the right ones. Consider that for good health and optimal body weight, the country's top nutrition experts recommend you get:

- 25 to 35 grams of fibre (found primarily in carbs) a day. Most people get fewer than 15.
- At least 10 grams of Resistant Starch (found primarily in carbs) a day. Most people get fewer than 4.
- 5 to 9 servings of fruit and vegetables a day. Most people eat fewer than 3.
- 3 servings of wholegrains a day. Most people don't even get 1.

3. I'm a carb addict! First, it's a little pasta. Then it's on to bagels, biscuits, cake!

Let's back up here. Real food addictions are actually kind of rare: Top experts in the field say they afflict a tiny subset of people, most of whom are severely obese. Even if this describes you, the substances addicts binge on (fatty, sugary, highly processed junk food) bear no resemblance whatsoever to the fresh, nutrient-packed, balanced meals you'll be eating on *The CarbLover's Diet*.

Ask the **carb pro**

Frances Largeman-Roth, RD

Q. Pasta really freaks me out. Any tips for making friends with this food again?

A. Sure! People mistakenly think "pasta" means piles of starch on a plate. You generally don't sit down to a gigantic mound of brown rice, right? Likewise, pasta should be enjoyed with other flavours and ingredients such as fresh herbs, vegetables, lean meats, interesting sauces and even nuts and beans. Experiment! Go for wholewheat pasta varieties, and try all the cool shapes out there like farfalle (bow tie), campanelle, fiori, gemelli and others.

4. So carbs are "in" now. What happens when they're "out" and low-carb is back "in"?

The nutrition science community has always endorsed a carb-rich diet as the best way to stay healthy and slim. As for Resistant Starch? There are hundreds of peer-reviewed, published studies supporting its benefits for health and weight loss (and none suggesting any downsides!). Bottom line: Carbs may be "in" now, but they're honestly here to stay.

5. My favourite celebs don't touch carbs!

You'll make yourself crazy comparing yourself to Hollywood stars, whose careers depend so much on keeping their size 0 figures that some **do** advocate pretty extreme diets, including fasting. *The CarbLover's Diet* was designed for real people who want to get slim and stay that way forever – without starving themselves.

6. Carbs don't fill me up like a good steak!

Whenever you hear people talking about filling foods, they usually mean protein. Yet carbs are the most satisfying foods you can eat (see Chapter 2 for the evidence). And they're the best feel-full bargain around: You can eat double or triple the amount of carbs compared to fat or protein for the same calories. But don't take my word for it – put carbs to the test. Eat them for breakfast (see our list of options on pages 94 and 116) for one week, and try bacon and eggs for another week. I bet you'll find, as I have, that carbs carry you through the day with way more energy and less hunger than other foods.

7. Bread makes me blow up overnight!

What you're talking about here is bloating, not weight gain, and you can't blame carbs for either. It takes an extra 3,500 calories to gain just 500 g (1 lb) pound, so unless you devoured more than 3 litres (5 pints) of full-fat ice cream after dinner, you could not possibly have gained weight overnight. Extra salt is what really makes you blow up, explains Frances Largeman-Roth, RD (my co-author). So if you went to the cinema, shared a tub of popcorn with a pal, and then had trouble zipping up your skinny jeans, blame the salt, not the corn! To get right back on track, drink extra water and go easy on packaged and processed foods for a few days.

8. I can't possibly start *CarbLover's* now. My (birthday, holiday, school reunion, you fill-in-the-blank) is coming up!

Sure you can. Because right now is the best time to lose weight, and there are so many options for doing it quickly and easily on *The CarbLover's Diet* – without sacrificing your lifestyle. You can have home-cooked family *CarbLover's* meals, at-your-desk lunches, dining-out options ... even fast-food choices. Go directly to Chapter 10 for even more details on being a *CarbLover* in any situation.

Your mood on carbs

People feel happier when they include carbs in their diets and crankier when they restrict them, but researchers don't know precisely why this is the case. One theory: Carbs boost the feel-good brain chemical serotonin. Another is that sweet, carb-rich foods elevate mood-boosting opiates in the brain, triggering pleasurable sensations.

"I Lost Weight on *CarbLover's*"

BEFORE

ROSEMARY SHMAVONIAN

Age: **48**
Height: **1.62 m (5' 4")**
Weight before: **74.8 kg (11 st 11 lb)**
Weight after: **70.3 kg (11 st 1 lb)**
Weight lost: **4.5 kg (10 lb)**

Biggest success moment:
I have a floral dress that my husband bought me years ago. It barely fitted when I got it, but I'm wearing it to a wedding this spring. And it looks great!

Biggest challenge: Finding the time to shop for food. But once I stocked my cabinets with barley, quinoa, and beans, I was set for months!

Favourite recipe: Cannellini Bean Salsa & Chips (page 199). It tastes like no diet food I've ever had!

AFTER

I never battled with my weight until after my two pregnancies. I had my boys in my late 30s, and losing 18 kg (40 lb) post-pregnancy was harder than I thought! I've tried low-carb diets like South Beach before, but I was hungry, cranky, and the scales didn't move. *CarbLover's* appealed to me because I needed a diet that fitted into our carb-eating family's lifestyle and not just mine. Since my husband has high cholesterol, the fibre in these recipes seemed like a healthy choice for him, too.

At first my weight loss was slow. But by week three, I had dropped 3.2 kg (7 lb). The weight just fell off my troublesome areas, like my stomach and hips. Even if the scales didn't move, I liked the way my body was changing shape.

Unlike other diets, this one emphasizes all the foods you **can** eat, instead of all the foods you can't. It's been surprisingly easy to craft meals, even when I've been travelling. At a recent breakfast buffet I went for *CarbLover's*-approved grits, smoked fish and fruit. It was delicious! I felt that I wasn't restricting food, but substituting all the junk I'd been eating with healthier foods. And there's nothing you absolutely can't have, which means I can stick with it! Incorporating *CarbLover's* ingredients like barley and quinoa into my day-to-day life has helped me drop 4.5 kg (10 lb) in two months. But more important, it's setting up healthy habits for my family.

PART

2

The *CarbLover's* Plan

Chapter 5

PHASE 1

The 7-Day *CarbLover's* Kickstart Plan

THE NEXT SEVEN DAYS WILL CHANGE YOUR LIFE FOREVER.
They make up the first phase of The CarbLover's Diet Plan. It is designed to help you lose up to 2.7 kg (6 lb) with minimal effort. What you do for the next week will also set the stage for even bigger achievements (including truly dramatic weight loss!) in Phase 2 of CarbLovers. Following this plan will improve your life in four ways you never dreamed possible:

1. Your longing for real food and feelings of deprivation will end forever because you'll be nourished with the foods your body has been hungry for ... maybe even since your childhood.

2. You'll feel more energized and in control than you have in years because you won't be skipping meals.

3. You'll relax *and* enjoy eating carbs again because you'll be losing weight on carb-rich foods.

4. You'll feel a whole lot happier because you'll finally be eating the carbs your body and brain craves – and you'll also be losing weight.

Favorite recipes: The sharp cheddar
& Egg on Rye * , and the Cherry
Ginger Scones * — the oatmeal
was tasty... must remember to
bring snack on Monday and
drink more water!

"Write down what you eat!
Keeping a food diary is
one of the best predictors
of weight loss."

IN THIS CHAPTER, you'll learn everything you need to drop real weight, real fast – without ever going hungry! We're going to give you seven days' worth of meals and snacks. You'll be able to enjoy delicious, easy recipes for breakfast, lunch and dinner and suggestions for prepared meals when you don't. Our 7-Day *CarbLover's* Kickstart Meal Plan starts on page 66 and includes advice from experts and real-life dieters to help you stay the course and lose weight.

The *CarbLover's* Kickstart Plan eases you into *CarbLover's* eating gently, so you'll never be tempted to stray. If you're still nervous about diving into a diet that puts carbs back on the plate, these three hallmarks of the plan will reassure you:

1. The 7-Day *CarbLover's* Kickstart Plan = 1,200 calories a day.

For the next seven days, you can simply follow the menu we've created – or you can mix and match the meals any way you choose. Either way, you'll lose that first 2 kilos or so. By the way, we understand if you're a little sceptical about the whole "carbs are my weight-loss friend" concept. Just know that whether you follow the menu to the letter or mix and match the meal choices, the 1,200 daily calories you get lead to only one outcome: rapid weight loss.

2. CarbLover's Kickstart was tested on real people.

Before we began to work on these menus, we recruited women of different ages, shapes and lifestyles to test our plan. Some were career-focused women, others were stay-at-home mums. Some had a lot of weight to lose, while others only wanted to drop a few kilos. But they did have one important thing in common: They all lost big on The 7-Day *CarbLover's* Kickstart Plan – from 1.4 kg (3 lb) to a whopping 2.7 kg (6 lb) in seven days! Most important, they gave us no-holds-barred feedback on what worked best for them. For example, some wanted foods they could share with their families, while others were eager for fast-food options. Some loved salads, while others were more interested in heartier fare. A couple of them started exercising on the diet and wanted a bit more food. Others were so satisfied that they actually wanted to eat less. We listened. With their input, we created a plan that not only guarantees weight loss, but is also flexible enough to work with any lifestyle. And the best news: All of our testers said they felt satisfied and filled with energy while they lost weight.

3. Anyone can stick to this plan.

The dietitians who designed these menus and recipes went the extra mile to keep them as simple as possible. The day-by-day *Carblover's* Kickstart Meal Plan eliminates guesswork, and even if you don't cook, you can easily follow along: There are plenty of no-cook choices as well as recipes.

THE 7-DAY *CARBLOVER'S* KICKSTART RULES (READ THIS BEFORE YOU START!)

● Don't cut out the carbs!

This plan puts you in control, but please – don't "adapt" it by cutting carbs. These foods were carefully designed to satisfy your cravings for brain- and body-nourishing nutrients that keep you feeling full. Cutting carbs will only trigger binges that keep you from your weight-loss goal.

● Do write down what you eat.

Keeping a food diary will help you lose weight and train you to incorporate carbs into your life again. University of Pittsburgh researchers found that dieters who consistently jotted down what they ate (and when) lost weight more quickly than dieters who didn't.[1] Researchers also found that keeping a food diary helped dieters follow their plans without backsliding or cheating, even after a full year. [2]

Keep your food diary either on paper or digitally (try the notes function on your mobile phone). As you jot down what you eat, place stars next to "Foods that are high in Resistant Starch" (see page 264 for a list), "Foods that boost metabolism" (see pages 266–267 for lists of foods that are rich in MUFAs, omega-3s, and more), and "Foods that are high in fibre." This way, you'll quickly commit to memory the foods that you should be eating from now on.

● Don't lean on artificial sweeteners.

Here's why I want you to ban the fake stuff on this diet: Studies suggest that artificial sweeteners (especially in diet drinks) don't promote weight loss and may even increase your cravings for sugary foods – thus helping you pack on pounds. Fake sweeteners are up to 600 times sweeter than sugar, but they aren't even real carbs! Consuming them every day numbs your taste buds to the natural sweetness of good-for-you carbs like bananas, berries and other fresh fruit.

● Prepare the same meals often.

Getting used to *CarbLover's* recipes serves a dual purpose. First, it's convenient. Themore often you make something, the easier it is for you to re-create. All of the *CarbLover's* Kickstart lunch and dinner options can be used during the 21-Day *CarbLover's* Immersion Plan and beyond, so it makes sense to get to know them. Eventually, you won't even need this book. You'll be able to shop for the right ingredients and create the meals on your own.

Second, we want you to be able to take this plan anywhere. Say you're on *CarbLover's* and you have to visit family across the country. If you're familiar with shopping for and assembling *CarbLover's* meals, you can stick to your diet in anyone's kitchen without a problem. They'll probably become converts to the diet just by trying your meals for a day or two!

● Eat one snack a day.

Snacking is important on this plan because having snacks prevents between-meal bingeing. But when you snack is up to you. If you're not sure when to have your snack, try it two to three hours after lunch. If you're a night owl, go ahead and have your mini-treat an hour or two after dinner. *Note:* It's fine to snack after breakfast, but most of our diet testers found that the longer they waited to eat their snack, the easier it was to stick to the diet.

Ask the carb pro
Frances Largeman-Roth, RD

Q. Can I eat breakfast for dinner – and vice versa – on *CarbLover's*?
A. Yes. Some people feel safer and more in control when they eat the same thing every day – even if it's a shake for dinner or pasta for breakfast! If that describes you, then go for it. It may make it easier for you to stick to the plan.

● Don't skip meals.

The 7-Day *CarbLover's* Kickstart Plan purposely includes breakfast, lunch, dinner and one snack. While lots of dieters take pride in their meal-skipping abilities, we don't want you to skip – EVER! You must stick to this pattern in order to maintain your blood sugar levels (and thus your energy) and keep hunger at bay. Skipping just one meal will make you feel tired and stressed – and more likely to pig out later.

● Keep trigger foods out of the house.

By the end of the 21-Day *CarbLover's* Immersion Plan in Chapter 6, you'll be able to consume carbs with confidence. But you're not there yet. So keep foods that make you act out-of-control crazy (mine is chocolate-chip cookie dough) out of the house, where they're less likely to make you lose your self-control.

● Don't drink liquid calories.

For the next seven days, you can drink water, coffee and tea (black, green or herbal, without sweeteners, but with up to 2 teaspoons of semi-skimmed milk) and my secret Fat-Flushing Cocktail (below). The Fat-Flushing Cocktail includes powerful metabolism-boosting ingredients that will help speed you to your goal. Skip fruit juice, alcoholic and carbonated beverages (even diet drinks or sparkling water), which make you look and feel bloated.

Fat-Flushing cocktail

Ellen Kunes, Editor in Chief *Health* Magazine

Shhh ... this drink is my secret, an all-natural diet aid that tastes great. The tea may help you burn off an extra 80 calories a day, and the citrus gives it a naturally sweet punch. Whether you want to share it is up to you.

2 litres (3½ pints) brewed green tea
Juice from 1 orange
Juice from 1 lemon
Juice from 1 lime

Mix all the ingredients together in one large jug. Serve hot or iced: store in the fridge for up to 3 days.

PHASE 1

The 7-Day *CarbLover's* Kickstart Meal plan

This plan makes eating the *CarbLover's* way a no-brainer. We've included at-a-glance meals, and even pre-prepared, restaurant and shop-bought options for dieters who don't have time to cook! Where there's room, we've written out the recipe in the menus – even when it appears again in Chapter 7 – so you don't have to flip pages. Feel free to mix and match any course in any menu, and don't even think about skipping meals!

7-DAY CARBLOVER'S KICKSTART PLAN

The 7-Day Checklist

- **Sit down to every meal:** Grabbing something and eating it over the sink sets you up for overeating. It doesn't give you a chance to be mindful about your food, and you're less likely to pay attention to the serving size. Sit down and enjoy!

- **Stay hydrated:** Sometimes we mistake thirst for hunger, so hydrate! Drink eight 240 ml (8-fl oz) glasses of water each day.

- **Tell the world you're on a diet:** OK, maybe not everyone, but telling a few close friends will help keep you honest and motivated.

- **Ditch distractions:** TV, music, and even dinner companions can cause you to overeat.

- **Slow down:** Try to relax and slow down while you eat. You'll enjoy your food more and will eat less!

- **Ban family-style:** Instead of putting out all of the *CarbLover's* recipe you cooked, portion out your plate and enjoy that amount. You'll eat less without feeling deprived.

- **Raid Grandma's china cabinet:** The dinner plates we use today are far bigger than they used to be. Pick up smaller ones from Grandma or find some at a car boot sale. Or try using your salad plate instead of your dinner plate. It will feel like you have a lot more food on your plate!

MONDAY (DAY 1)

Breakfast
Banana Shake (page 99): Blend 1 banana, 350 ml (12 fl oz) 1% semi-skimmed milk, 2 teaspoons honey and 120 ml (4 fl oz) ice
or
Nature Valley Chewy Trail Mix Bar plus 1 banana

Lunch
Chicken Pitta Sandwich (page 102): 40 g (1½ oz) baby spinach, ½ sliced red pepper and 125 g (4 oz) cooked skinless, boneless chicken strips, tossed with 2 tablespoons low-fat Italian vinaigrette, and stuffed into 1 (15 cm/6-inch) wholemeal pitta (halved)

Dinner
Griddled Salmon & Parmesan Potatoes (page 112)
or
Linda McCartney Spinach and Soya Mince Cannelloni

Snack
Greek yogurt (180 ml/6 fl oz) natural low-fat) plus honey (2 teaspoons) plus rolled oats (2 tablespoons, uncooked or toasted)

TUESDAY (DAY 2)

Breakfast
Banana-Nut Porridge (page 96)
or
1 banana plus 1 teaspoon peanut or almond butter

Lunch
Express Lunch Plate (page 103)
1 large hard-boiled egg, 25 g (1 oz) Cheddar cheese and 1 sliced apple, served with 3 rye crackers

Dinner
Prawn Stir-Fry with Ginger (page 111)
or
2 Linda McCartney Vegetarian Burgers with 1 toasted wholemeal bun and 1 teaspoon mustard plus 1 medium apple

Snack
Cannellini & Herb Hummus with Crudités (page 115): 65 g (2½ oz) canned white beans (rinsed and drained) mashed with 2 teaspoons olive oil, 1 tablespoon chopped chives and 1 tablespoon lemon juice. Serve dip with 75 g (3 oz) sliced raw vegetables

WEDNESDAY (DAY 3)

Breakfast
Banana Shake Plus (page 99):
Blend 1 banana, 350 ml (12 fl oz) 1% fat milk, 2 teaspoons honey, 120 ml (4 fl oz) ice, and 2 teaspoons ground flaxseed

Lunch
Big Chopped Salad (page 100)

Dinner
Black Bean Tacos (page 104)
or
200 g (7 oz) Baxters Healthy Minestrone with Wholemeal Pasta with 3 rye crackers

Snack
Salsa (2 tablespoons) plus canned black beans (2 tablespoons, rinsed and drained), served with corn tortilla chips (8)

THURSDAY (DAY 4)

Breakfast
Banana-Berry Shake (page 99):
Blend 1 banana, 350 ml (12 fl oz) 1%
fat milk, 2 teaspoons honey, 120 ml
(4 fl oz) ice and 40 g (1½ oz) berries
or
Nature Valley Chewy Trail Mix Bar
plus 1 banana

Lunch
Chicken Pitta Sandwich (page
102): 40 g (1½ oz) baby spinach, ½
sliced red pepper, and 125 g (4 oz)
cooked skinless, boneless chicken
strips, tossed with 2 tablespoons
low-fat Italian vinaigrette, and stuffed
into a 15 cm (6-inch) wholemeal pitta
(halved)
or
2 Linda McCartney Vegetarian
Burgers with 1 toasted wholemeal bun
and 1 teaspoon mustard plus 1
medium apple

Dinner
Chicken Pasta Primavera
(page 107)
or
Linda McCartney Spinach and Soya
Mince Cannelloni

Snack
Almond butter (2 teaspoons) with 2
rye crackers

FRIDAY (DAY 5)

Breakfast
Banana & Almond Butter Toast
(page 95): 1 toasted slice of rye
bread topped with 1 tablespoon
almond butter and 1 sliced banana
or
40 g (1½ oz) Kellog's All-Bran cereal
with 120 ml (4 fl oz) 1% fat milk and
½ sliced banana

Lunch
Express Lunch Plate (page 103):
1 large hard-boiled egg, 25 g (1 oz)
Cheddar cheese and 1 sliced apple,
served with 3 rye crackers
or
Linda McCartney Spinach and Soya
Mince Cannelloni

Dinner
Grilled Burger & 3-Bean Salad
(page 108)
or
Young's It's in the Bag Salmon Pasta
plus 175 g (6 oz) salad leaves with
low-fat vinaigrette

Snack
Trail Mix (page 114):
cornflakes (15 g/½ oz) flaked
almonds (2 tablespoons) plus dried
cherries (2 tablespoons)

SATURDAY (DAY 6)

Breakfast
Banana-Cocoa Shake (page 99):
Blend 1 banana, 350 ml (12 fl oz)
1% fat milk, 2 teaspoons honey,
120 ml (4 fl oz) ice, and 1 tablespoon
unsweetened cocoa

or

Nature Valley Chewy Trail Mix Bar
plus 1 banana

Lunch
Big Chopped Salad (page 100)

or

200 g (7 oz) Baxters Healthy
Minestrone with Wholemeal Pasta
with 3 rye crackers

Dinner
**Fish Tacos with Sesame-Ginger
Coleslaw** (page 172)

or

200 g (7 oz) Baxters Healthy
Minestrone with Wholemeal Pasta
with 3 rye crackers

Snack
Greek yogurt (180 ml/6 fl oz, natural/
low-fat) plus honey (2 teaspoons) plus
rolled oats (2 tablespoons, uncooked
or toasted)

SUNDAY (DAY 7)

Breakfast
Banana & Almond Butter Toast
(page 95): 1 toasted slice of rye
bread topped with 1 tablespoon
almond butter and 1 sliced banana

or

40 g (1½ oz) Kellogg's All-Bran cereal
with 120 ml (4 fl oz) 1% fat milk and
½ sliced banana

Lunch
Express Lunch Plate (page 103):
1 large hard-boiled egg, 25 g (1 oz)
cheddar cheese and 1 sliced apple,
served with 3 rye crackers

or

Young's It's in the Bag Salmon Pasta
plus 175 g (6 oz) salad leaves with
low-fat vinaigrette

Dinner
**Grilled Salmon & Parmesan
Potatoes** (page 112)

or

2 Linda McCartney Vegetarian
Burgers with 1 toasted wholemeal
bun and 1 teaspoon mustard plus
1 medium apple

Snack
Baked potato crisps (24 crisps, about
25 g/1 oz)

"I Lost Weight on *CarbLover's*"

BEFORE

CAITLIN GRAMS
....

Age: 24
Height: 1.6 m (5' 3")
**Weight before: 69.9 kg
(11 st)**
**Weight after: 65.8 kg
(10 st 5lb)**
Weight lost: 4.1 kg (9 lb)

....

Biggest success moment: Fitting
into a pair of skinny jeans I'd been
eyeing.
Biggest challenge: Facing
my fear of rice, pasta and bread!
CarbLover's really helped me
overcome my carbo-phobia!
Favourite recipe: Dark Chocolate
& Oat Clusters (page 213). Two of
these clusters completely satisfy my
sweet tooth, and my husband LOVES
them.

AFTER

It's ironic and eye-opening that I had success on **The CarbLover's Diet** because I was someone who always banned rice, passed on the bread basket and limited pasta, which was difficult when I married into an Italian family!

I've been overweight most of my life. Though I've always been a runner, I was never good at portion control. About three years ago, I hit my heaviest weight, 83.9 kg (13 st 3 lb). I tried other diets, but they seemed so boring and gimmicky after a while.

CarbLover's seemed different but I was a little afraid I would be hungry, especially during Phase 1. But after two or three days of eating the wholegrains, I realized I wasn't starving at all. I'm not a huge lunch person, but this diet forced me to eat it. I always thought salads were dull, but the chopped salad on this diet combined chickpeas and red cabbage – two things I never would have added to my greens!

In the past I felt as if I always needed more sleep, but on **CarbLover's** I slept the same amount and had more energy throughout the day. My fitness goal was to run two 6-mile loops in Central Park. The foods I ate on **CarbLover's** fuelled my runs and gave me the energy to achieve my goal!

In two months, I've lost 4.1 kg (9 lb) and feel completely in control of my eating habits.

Chapter 6

The 21-Day *CarbLover's* Immersion Plan

BY NOW YOU'RE PROBABLY AT LEAST 2.5 KG (5½ LB) LIGHTER, and you're enjoying a new, healthier relationship with yummy foods you haven't eaten in a long time. Best of all, you're bursting with energy! It's time to take your slimmed-down self and get ready for the next phase of CarbLover's because the best is yet to come. In Phase 2 of *The CarbLover's Diet,* called The 21-Day CarbLover's Immersion Plan, you'll be adding even more favourite foods (think steak and potato dinners, French toast for breakfast, even the occasional chocolate treat). Portion sizes will increase, and you'll be able to order from the menu at your favourite restaurants.

You'll eat all this, and you'll still lose another 2.7 kg (6 lb) – or even more. On The 21-Day *CarbLover's* Immersion Plan, you actually get to eat 1,600 calories a day (up from the 1,200 calories you had on The 7-Day *CarbLover's* Kickstart Plan). Losing weight gets even easier during this part of *CarbLover's* because The 21-Day *CarbLover's* Immersion Plan is designed to fit in perfectly with your unique lifestyle. Before you dive into the menu and meal plan, check out how to make it work best for you.

YOU HAVE TWO GREAT OPTIONS HERE:

1. You can build your own customized daily menus by mixing and matching meal choices from our CarbLover's Recipe Collection (starting on page 93).

2. Or for those of you who prefer more guidance, we've created a 21-day meal plan you'll absolutely love, starting on page 78. These menus were developed by our dietitians and tested on a group of incredibly busy women. They told us this plan was easy to follow – and that not having to create their own menus every day made losing weight 100 per cent stress-free.

Most important: **All *CarbLover's* meals are interchangeable,** and any combination will help you lose weight. Eat the same thing for breakfast every day, if that keeps it easy for you – or eat one of our dinners for lunch or a favourite breakfast for dinner, if you feel like it. It all adds up to fat-burning and weight loss!

YOUR GOALS FOR THE NEXT THREE WEEKS ARE TO:

● **Lose about 1 kg (2 lb) each week.** By the end of the *CarbLover's* Kickstart and CarbLover's Immersion Phases, most dieters say they've lost a total of at least 5 kg (11 lb) – without feeling hungry!

● **Relax and enjoy eating carbs!** You've now got proof that you can eat bread, rice, pasta and more without fear.

● **Know how to spot appetite-suppressors** like fibre, Resistant Starch and MUFAs in prepared foods – and make smart choices if you stray from the plan.

● **Feel confident** about converting *CarbLover's* from a diet to a way of life. At the end of three weeks, preparing *CarbLover's* meals will become second nature.

HOW IS THE 21-DAY *CARBLOVER'S* IMMERSION PLAN DIFFERENT FROM THE KICKSTART PLAN?

● You get to eat more!

You'll get larger portions than you did during The *7-Day CarbLover's* Kickstart Plan. Many of our test dieters told us that they were so satisfied with these meals that they could not finish what was on their plates. We actually had to coach them to eat their snacks!

● You get lots of choices!

This plan includes super-satisfying meals, decadent treats and fast food and/or restaurant options that appeal to every palate. You won't feel as if you are on a diet so you'll have a much easier time sticking with the plan.

● You get plenty of treats!

Dessert! Wine! Cappuccino! Every day, you get to choose two snacks (compared to one on The *7-Day CarbLover's* Kickstart Plan), and one of these snacks can be an indulgence chosen from the list provided on page 116. From ice cream and chocolate-covered bananas to sweet potato pudding, you won't believe what you can enjoy and still lose weight!

This is diet food? You bet. On *CarbLover's*, treats are on the menu!

PHASE 2

The 21-Day *CarbLover's* Immersion Meal plan

TO GET YOU STARTED on the next phase of *CarbLover's*, here are three weeks of menu suggestions. We've included plenty of options for alternative meals to be prepared at home. Where there's room, we've written out the recipe in the menus – even when it appears again in Chapter 7 – so you don't have to flip pages if you're in a hurry. Feel free to mix and match any meal in any menu!

21-Day Checklist

- **Keep track of snacks:** If you run or walk more than 8 km (5 miles) a day and/or you start to feel really hungry or tired, go ahead and double the size of one of your snacks. If you're not losing weight at all, cut one out.

- **When you feel full, stop eating!** Don't feel that you should clean your plate. The suggested portions in the menu options and recipes are just that – suggestions. Many of our test dieters said that portions were sometimes too big for them. If you feel too full after meals, scale back.

- **Mix and match:** Incorporate your favourite menu options from The 7-Day *CarbLover's* Kickstart Plan into The 21-Day CarbLover's Immersion Plan. All of the meal options from Phase 1 of our diet will also work during Phase 2.

MONDAY (Day 1)

Breakfast
Breakfast Barley with Banana & Sunflower Seeds (page 119): Mix 75 g (3 oz) quick-cooking barley with 150 ml (5 fl oz) water and microwave for 6 minutes. Let stand for 2 minutes, then top with 1 teaspoon honey, 1 sliced banana and 1 tablespoon sunflower seeds.
or
Banana Berry Shake (page 99)

Lunch
Ham, Sliced Pear & Swiss Sandwich (page 146)
or
Express Lunch Plate (page 103)

Dinner
Roasted Pork Fillet with Apricot-Barley Pilaf (page 186)
or
Seared Chicken Breasts with French Potato Salad (page 185)

Snack #1
Antipasto Platter (page 209): 12 canned black olives (drained), 8 tablespoons marinated artichoke hearts (drained) and ½ red pepper (sliced).

Snack #2
25 g (1 oz) dark chocolate-covered cherries (about 3)

TUESDAY (Day 2)

Breakfast
Banana Yogurt Parfait with Maple Oat Topping (page 118)
or
Porridge with Prune & Banana Compote (page 128)

Lunch
Tuscan Barley Salad (page 165)
or
Pesto Turkey Club (page 158)

Dinner
Sirloin Salad with Blue Cheese Dressing & Sweet Potato Chips (page 181)
or
Griddled Salmon & Parmesan Potatoes (page 112)

Snack #1
Pistachio & Dried Cherry Crostini (page 209): 2 tablespoons low-fat cottage cheese mixed with 1 teaspoon honey, 2 teaspoons chopped pistachios and 2 teaspoons chopped dried cherries, served on top of 2 rye crackers.

Snack #2
10 chocolate-covered peanuts

WEDNESDAY (Day 3)

Breakfast
Tomato & Mozzarella Melt (page 136)
or
Cornflakes, Low-Fat Milk & Berries (page 127)

Lunch
Big Chopped Salad (page 100)
or
Roast Beef Sandwich with Horseradish Aioli (page 161): serve with 150 g (5 oz) sliced cucumber and 1 tablespoon light Italian dressing

Dinner
Barley Risotto Primavera (page 166)
or
Spanish-Style Prawns with Yellow Rice (page 182)

Snack #1
Brie and apple slices (page 209): 1 small sliced apple with 25 g (1 oz) Brie.

Snack #2
One glass of red wine (150 ml/5 fl oz)

THURSDAY (Day 4)

Breakfast
Broccoli & Feta Omelette with Toast (page 122)

or

Toast with Walnut & Pear Breakfast Spread (page 129)

Lunch
Pesto Turkey Club (page 158) and 1 apple

or

Mediterranean Pasta Salad (page 150)

Dinner
Fish Tacos with Sesame-Ginger Slaw (page 172)

or

Seared Chicken Breasts with French Potato Salad (page 185)

Snack #1
Fig & Flax Yogurt (page 209): Mix 120 ml (4 fl oz) low-fat natural Greek yogurt with 1 teaspoon honey, 3 dried, chopped figs and 1 teaspoon ground flaxseeds.

Snack #2
Grande (500 ml/16 oz) cappuccino, with semi-skimmed milk

FRIDAY (Day 5)

Breakfast
Cheddar & Egg on Rye (page 134)

or

Apple & Almond Muesli (page 177)

Lunch
Roast Beef Sandwich with Horseradish Aioli (page 161). Serve with 150 g (5 oz) sliced cucumber and 1 tablespoon light Italian dressing.

or

Express Lunch Plate (page 103)

Dinner
Mediterranean Seafood Grill with Skordalia (page 175)

or

Chicken Pasta Primavera (page 107)

Snack #1
Greek Yogurt with Marmalade & Walnuts (page 209): 120 ml (4 fl oz) low-fat natural Greek yogurt mixed with 2 teaspoons 100% fruit marmalade and 1 tablespoon chopped walnuts

Snack #2
Chocolate-Orange Spoonbread (page 214)

SATURDAY (Day 6)

Breakfast
Cherry-Ginger Scones (page 125)
or
Coconut French Toast Raspberry Syrup
(page 126)l

Lunch
Black Bean & Courgette Quesadillas (page 141)
or
Middle Eastern Rice Salad (page 153)

Dinner
Baked Two-Cheese Penne with Roasted Red Pepper Sauce
(page 192)
or
Sirloin Salad with Blue Cheese
Dressing & Sweet Potato Crisps
(page 181)

Snack #1
Honey-Curried Yogurt Dip with Carrots & Broccoli (page 209):
Mix 120 ml (4 fl oz) low-fat natural
Greek yogurt with 1 teaspoon honey,
1/4 teaspoon curry powder and
1/8 teaspoon salt. Serve with 125 g
(4 oz) each of baby carrots and
broccoli florets.

Snack #2
Dark Chocolate & Oat Clusters
(page 213)

SUNDAY (Day 7)

Breakfast
Potato-Crusted Spinach Quiche
(page 133)
or
Courgette & Potato Scramble with
Bacon (page 137)

Lunch
Rocket Salad with Lemon Dijon Dressing (page 138)
or
Moroccan Chicken Pitta (page 154)

Dinner
Thai Peanut Noodles (page 190)
or
Roasted Vegetable & Italian Sausage
with Polenta (page 189)

Snack #1
Hummus with Feta & Dill
(page 209): Top 4 tablespoons
hummus (shop-bought tub) with
1 tablespoon feta cheese and
1/8 teaspoon dried dill. Serve with
150 g (5 oz) sliced cucumber.

Snack #2
25 g (1 oz) plain chocolate

21-Day Checklist (continued)

● **Prevent plateaus:** If your weight-loss stalls during The 21-Day *CarbLover's* Immersion Plan, you can go back to The 7-Day *CarbLover's* Kickstart Plan to jump-start your diet again. You will lose all the weight you want on *CarbLover's*, it just might take you a bit longer.

● **Don't skip meals or snacks in an attempt to speed up your pounds-off results:** Doing so will backfire by triggering cravings. If you really think you're eating too much food, shrink your portions slightly. But whatever you do, don't skip meals!

● **Go bananas:** These menus have been created to ensure you consume at least 10 grams of Resistant Starch a day. Bananas are a big part of that secret formula because they contain more Resistant Starch than any other single food (4.7 grams, and even more for a green one!). But if you are simply tired of bananas (or out of them), eat any medium-sized piece of fruit or 125 g (4 oz) of berries.

MONDAY (Day 8)

Breakfast
Porridge with Prune & Banana Compote (page 128)
or
Banana & Almond Butter Toast (page 95)

Lunch
Middle Eastern Rice Salad (page 153)
or
Greek Lentil Soup with Toasted Pitta (page 145)

Dinner
Spanish-Style Prawns with Yellow Rice (page 182)
or
Orecchiette with Cannellini Beans & Pesto (page 177)

Snack #1
Salmon & Cream Cheese Bites (page 209): Spread 2 teaspoons low-fat cream cheese on 1 slice toasted pumpernickel bread. Top with 15 g (½ oz) smoked salmon and 2 teaspoons chopped chives.

Snack #2
10 chocolate-covered peanuts

TUESDAY (Day 9)

Breakfast
Cornflakes, Low-Fat Milk & Berries (page 127): 50 g (2 oz) cornflakes served with 240 ml (8 fl oz) low-fat milk and topped with 125 g (4 oz) fresh or thawed frozen berries.
or
Cheddar & Egg on Rye (page 134)

Lunch
Smoked Salmon & Avocado Rolls (page 162)
or
Tuscan Barley Salad (page 165)

Dinner
Pan-Seared Scallops with Mexican Rice Salad (page 178)
or
Black Bean Tacos (page 104)

Snack #1
Cheddar & Apple Melt (page 208): Place 1 tablespoon grated cheddar cheese and 1 small thinly sliced apple in 1 corn tortilla. Microwave for 30 seconds until cheese is bubbling.

Snack #2
1 serving low-fat ice cream

WEDNESDAY (Day 10)

Breakfast
Apple & Almond Muesli (page 117): Combine 50 g (2 oz) rolled oats with 120 ml (4 fl oz) low-fat milk, and let sit for 5 to 10 minutes. Stir in 1 chopped apple, 2 tablespoons flaked almonds and 2 teaspoons honey.
or
Banana-Nut Porridge (page 96)

Lunch
Express Lunch Plate (page 103): 1 hard-boiled egg, 25 g (1 oz) Cheddar cheese, and 1 sliced apple served with 3 rye crackers.
or
Indian Chicken Salad with Peanuts (page 149)

Dinner
Caribbean Mahi Mahi with Banana Chutney (page 171)
or
Barley Risotto Primavera (page 166)

Snack #1
Chilli-Spiked Pitta Chips (page 202)

Snack #2
Banana Ice Cream (page 210)

THURSDAY (Day 11)

Breakfast
Courgette & Potato Scramble with Bacon (page 137)
or
Banana Shake (page 99)

Lunch
Moroccan Chicken Pitta (page 154)
or
Red Grape & Tuna Salad Pitta (page 159)

Dinner
Orecchiette with Cannellini Beans & Pesto (page 177)
or
Pan-Seared Scallops with Mexican Rice Salad (page 178)

Snack #1
Pea & Walnut Hummus (page 198)

Snack #2
Chocolate-Dipped Banana Bites (page 212): Melt 2 tablespoons plain chocolate chips. Dip 1 small banana (peeled and cut into 2.5 cm/1 inch chunks) in the chocolate.

FRIDAY (Day 12)

Breakfast
Porridge with Prune & Banana Compote (page 128): Microwave 50 g (2 oz) rolled oats with 240 ml (8 fl oz) low-fat milk for 3 to 5 minutes (according to packet instructions). Top with 3 chopped prunes, 1 diced banana and 1 tablespoon chopped crystallized ginger.
or
Apple & Almond Muesli (page 117)

Lunch
Curried Egg Salad Sandwich (page 142) plus 1 orange
or
Pesto Turkey Club (page 158)

Dinner
Bistro-Style Steak with New Potatoes (page 168)
or
Thai Peanut Noodles (page 190)

Snack #1
Creamy Sweet Potato Dip (page 204)

Snack #2
Quick Mango-Coconut Sorbet (page 216)

SATURDAY (Day 13)

Breakfast
Coconut French Toast with Raspberry Syrup (page 126)
or
Cornflakes, Low-Fat Milk & Berries (page 127)

Lunch
Chicken Pitta Sandwich (page 102): Toss 40 g (1½ oz) baby spinach, ½ sliced red pepper, and 125 g (4 oz) cooked boneless, skinless chicken strips with 2 tablespoons low-fat Italian vinaigrette. Stuff into 1 (15 cm/6 inch) wholemeal pitta (halved).
or
Rocket Salad with Lemon-Dijon Dressing (page 138)

Dinner
Bacon, Pear & Gorgonzola Pizza (page 194)
or
Mediterranean Seafood Grill with Skordalia (page 175)

Snack #1
Cannellini Bean Salsa and Chips (page 199)

Snack #2
Raspberries with Chocolate Yogurt Mousse (page 224)

SUNDAY (Day 14)

Breakfast
Broccoli & Feta Omelette with Toast (page 122)
or
Blueberry Pancakes with Maple Yoghurt (page 120)

Lunch
Greek Lentil Soup with Toasted Pitta (page 145)
or
Tuscan Barley Salad (page 165)

Dinner
Baked Two-Cheese Penne with Roasted Red Pepper Sauce (page 192)
or
Grilled Burger & Three-Bean Salad (page 108)

Snack #1
Antipasto Platter (page 209): 12 canned black olives (drained), 8 tablespoons marinated artichoke hearts (drained), and ½ red pepper (sliced).

Snack #2
Dark Chocolate & Oat Clusters (page 213)

The 21-Day *CarbLover's* Immersion Plan **85**

21-Day Checklist Continued

- **Don't be a slave (to your stove):** When life gets busy, opt for a take-away or a restaurant meal (see page 259 for suitable suggestions).

- **Try exercising – even if you didn't before!** Carb-rich foods (such as those in our recipes in Chapter 7) slow digestion, which keeps glucose – the body's main energy source – pumping into your cells steadily. End result: Your energy never lags. No more sluggish afternoons and lots more stamina for exercise.

MONDAY (Day 15)

Breakfast
Polenta Fritters with Asparagus & Eggs (page 130)
or
Tomato & Mozzarella Melt (page 136)

Lunch
Pecan-Crusted Goat's Cheese Salad with Pomegranate Vinaigrette
(page 157)
or
Red Grape & Tuna Salad Pitta
(page 159)

Dinner
Roasted Vegetables & Italian Sausage with Polenta (page 189)
or
Fish Tacos with Sesame Ginger Coleslaw (page 172)

Snack #1
Coconut-Date Truffles (page 196)

Snack #2:
Maple Brown Rice Pudding
(page 219)

TUESDAY (Day 16)

Breakfast
Toast with Walnut & Pear Breakfast Spread (page 129): Blend 125 g (4 oz) low-fat cottage cheese until smooth. Stir in 1 tablespoon chopped walnuts and 1 diced pear. Serve on 2 slices toasted sourdough bread.
or
Banana-Nut Porridge (page 96)

Lunch
Pesto Turkey Club (page 158): Spread 2 teaspoons prepared pesto onto 2 slices pumpernickel bread. Add 25 g (1 oz) sliced turkey, 1 slice cooked turkey bacon, 2 cos lettuce leaves and 4 slices tomato. Serve with 1 apple.
or
Mediterranean Pesto Salad (page 150)

Dinner
Seared Chicken Breasts with French Potato Salad (page 185)
or
Spanish-style Prawns with Yellow Rice (page 182)

Snack #1
Garlic & Herb Yogurt Dip (page 201)

Snack #2
Merlot Strawberries with Whipped Cream (page 220)

WEDNESDAY (Day 17)

Breakfast
Apple & Almond Muesli (page 117): Combine 50 g (2 oz) rolled oats and 120 ml (4 fl oz) 1% fat milk in a small bowl. Let stand for 5 to 10 minutes. Stir in 1 chopped apple, 2 tablespoons flaked almonds and 2 teaspoons honey.
or
Courgette & Potato Scramble with Bacon (page 137)

Lunch
Roast Beef Sandwich with Horseradish Aïoli (page 161) plus 150 g (5 oz) sliced cucumber drizzled with 1 tablespoon low-fat Italian dressing.
or
Rocket Salad with Lemon-Dijon Dressing (page 138)

Dinner
Thai Peanut Noodles (page 190)
or
Chicken Pasta Primavera (page 107)

Snack #1
Sunflower Lentil Spread (page 203)

Snack #2
Sweet Potato Pudding (page 222)

The 21-Day *CarbLover's* Immersion Plan **87**

THURSDAY (Day 18)

Breakfast
Cornflakes, Low-Fat Milk & Berries (page 127): Combine 50 g (2 oz) cornflakes and 240 ml (8 fl oz) 1% fat milk in a small bowl. Top with 125 g (4 oz) fresh or thawed frozen berries.

or

Polenta Fritters with Asparagus & Eggs (page 130)

Lunch
Red Grape & Tuna Salad Pitta (page 159)

or

Big Chopped Salad (page 100)

Dinner
Grilled Burger & Three-Bean Salad (page 108)

or

Baked Two-Cheese Penne with Roasted Red Pepper Sauce (page 192)

Snack #1
Creamy Sweet Potato Dip (page 204)

Snack #2
1 glass of red wine (150 ml/5 oz)

FRIDAY (Day 19)

Breakfast
Porridge with Prune & Banana Compote (page 128): Combine 240 ml (8 fl oz) 1% fat milk and 50 g (2 oz) rolled oats in a small microwave-safe bowl. Microwave on HIGH for 3 to 5 minutes (according to packet directions). Top with 3 chopped prunes, 1 diced banana and 1 tablespoon chopped crystallized ginger.

or

Banana Cocoa Shake (page 99)

Lunch
Moroccan Chicken Pitta (page 154)

or

Ham, Sliced Pear & Cheese Sandwich (page 146)

Dinner
Prawn Stir-Fry with Ginger (page 111)

or

Sirloin Salad with Blue Cheese Dressing & Sweet Potato Chips (page 181)

Snack #1
Warm Pear with Cinnamon Ricotta (page 207)

Snack #2
25 g (1 oz) plain chocolate

SATURDAY (Day 20)

Breakfast
Cheddar & Egg on Rye
(page 134)
or
Cherry Ginger Scones (page 125)

Lunch
Indian Chicken Salad with Peanuts (page 149)
or
Smoked Salmon & Avocado Rolls
(page 162)

Dinner
Bacon, Pear & Gorgonzola Pizza
(page 194)
or
Black Bean Tacos (page 104)

Snack #1
Cannellini Bean Salsa and Chips
(page 199)

Snack #2
Tall (360 ml/12 fl oz) latte with
semi-skimmed milk

SUNDAY (Day 21)

Breakfast
Blueberry Oat Pancakes with Maple Yogurt (page 120)
or
Breakfast Barley with Banana &
Sunflower Seeds (page 119)

Lunch
Curried Egg Salad Sandwich
(page 142) plus 1 orange
or
Pesto Turkey CLub (page 158)

Dinner
Griddled Salmon & Potatoes
(page 112)
or
Roasted Pork Fillet with Apricot-Barley
Pilaf (page 186)

Snack #1
Pistachio & Dried Cherry Crostini
(page 209): Combine 2 tablespoons
low-fat cottage cheese, 2 teaspoons
chopped pistachios, 2 teaspoons
chopped dried cherries and 1 teaspoon
honey. Serve on 2 rye crackers.

Snack #2
Chocolate-Dipped Banana Bites
(page 212): Melt 2 tablespoons plain
chocolate chips. Dip 1 small banana
(peeled and cut into 2.5 cm/1 inch
chunks) in melted chocolate.

The *CarbLover's* Kickstart Plan **89**

"I Lost Weight on *CarbLover's*"

BEFORE

CHRISTY ELLINGER

Age: 38
Height: 1.72 m (5' 8")
Weight before: 72.1 kg
(11 st 5 lb)
Weight after: 68 kg
(10 st 10 lb)
Weight lost: 4.1 kg (9 lb)

Biggest success: Seeing results away from the scales. I've lost 26 cm (10½ inches), and my body is more toned.

Biggest challenge: Restaurant portions. *CarbLover's* taught me that meals in restaurants are too big. Now, if I order a steak, I'll eat half and take the rest home for later.

Favourite recipe: The Sirloin Salad with Blue Cheese Dressing & Sweet Potato Chips (page 181) – I love how indulgent that dinner is – beef, cheese and chips just don't seem like diet food!

AFTER

I grew up eating food that wasn't healthy, and from time to time in my teen years I was an emotional eater: I didn't pay attention to what I was eating or drinking, and my weight would yo-yo.

As I got older it started to catch up with me. I was able to lose 9 kg (20 lb) in college, but I hit a plateau, and ever since, I've found myself fighting to keep it from sneaking back on

I tried a high-protein, low-carb diet for a week and felt disgusting from all the meat. I tried a shake-based diet, and I lost a lot of weight very quickly. Though I was happy with the results, I thought, 'Do I want to have shakes every day for the rest of my life?' No. I wanted a diet I could live with: Something that would keep those last persistent pounds off for good, and something sustainable.

I loved that *CarbLover's* wasn't very different from how I already ate. It simply taught me to look at the food on my plate before I eat, and make sure I've got the proportions right.

CarbLover's is great because it's not regimented. If I don't like a food, I don't have to eat it. And if there's something I want, nothing's off limits. If I want dessert, I have dessert! That kind of freedom made it easy for me. On top of that, I got the results I wanted. In just 12 weeks I lost 4.1 kg (9 lb). I feel like this plan is not just about short-term results – this is something I can incorporate into my everyday lifestyle.

Chapter 7

The *CarbLover's* Recipe Collection

WELCOME TO A NEW WORLD of delicious, real food. Meals you can look forward to each and every day for the rest of your life. Say goodbye forever to portions so small that your dinner was over and done with in just three bites, goodbye to snacks like rice cakes or even a handful of almonds (that never quite did it for me, either). In the following pages, you'll find over 75 breakfast, lunch, dinner, snack and dessert recipes. These sophisticated dishes are big on flavour, satisfaction and metabolism-boosting oomph, but they are small on prep time and cost.

7-DAY CARBLOVER'S KICKSTART RECIPES

BREAKFAST
Banana & Almond Butter Toast,
    page 95
Banana-Nut Porridge, page 96
Banana Shake, page 99

LUNCH
Big Chopped Salad, page 100
Chicken Pitta Sandwich, page 102
Express Lunch Plate, page 103

DINNER
Black Bean Tacos, page 104
Chicken Pasta Primavera, page 107
Grilled Burger & Three-Bean Salad, page 108
Prawn Stir-Fry with Ginger, page 111
Griddled Salmon & Parmesan Potatoes, page 112

SNACKS
Potato Crisps, page 114
Black Beans & Chips, page 114
Trail Mix, page 114
Greek Yogurt Parfait, page 114
Almond Butter Crackers, page 114
Cannellini & Herb Hummus with Crudités, page 115

HALLMARKS OF CARBLOVER'S RECIPES

● **They're loaded with Resistant Starch.** Main-course recipes include an average 3 grams of Resistant Starch (RS) each, and snacks average about 1 gram, making it easy for you to mix and match meals to hit your daily 10-gram target. (Look for RS in the nutritional analysis and in a yellow burst on the page.)

● **Most of our recipes can be prepared in 20 minutes or less**. In fact, some take no time to make at all.

● **They don't require special ingredients.** Nearly every item can be found at a food shop near you – no matter where you live.

● **They are affordable.** The ingredients used fit the budgets of even the most cost-conscious shopper.

Banana & Almond Butter Toast

This breakfast option couldn't be simpler, but it packs a nutritional wallop. The rye bread and banana will get you halfway to your daily Resistant Starch goal, and the almond butter adds metabolism-boosting MUFAs.

Prep: 5 minutes
Total time: 5 minutes
Makes: 1 serving

Resistant Starch:

5.6g

1 tablespoon almond butter
1 slice rye bread, toasted
1 banana, sliced

1. Spread almond butter on toast.

2. Top with banana slices.

Serving size: 1 piece of toast Calories 280; Fat 11g (sat 1g, mono 7g, poly 2.5g); Cholesterol 0mg; Protein 6g; Carbohydrate 44g; Sugars 16g; Fibre 5g; RS 5.6g; Sodium 260mg

Banana-Nut Porridge

By combining Resistant Starch powerhouses – banana and oats – this morning meal alone gets you halfway to your Resistant Starch goal of 10 daily grams. The walnuts add some omega-3s, too, for extra fat-burning.

Prep: 5 minutes
Cook: 5 minutes
Total time: 10 minutes
Makes: 1 serving

Resistant Starch:
5.2g

50 g (2 oz) rolled oats
240 ml (8 fl oz) water
1 banana, sliced
1 tablespoon chopped walnuts
1 teaspoon cinnamon

1. Combine oats and the water in a small microwave-safe bowl. Microwave at HIGH 3 minutes.

2. Top with banana slices, walnuts and cinnamon.

Serving size: 350 ml (12 fl oz) Calories 310; Fat 8g (sat 1g, mono 1.5g, poly 4.5g); Cholesterol 0mg; Protein 8g; Carbohydrate 57g; Sugars 16g; Fibre 9g; RS 5.2g; Sodium 0mg

★CarbStar★
PORRIDGE
4.6 grams of Resistant Starch per 50 g (2 oz) dry or toasted oats

Porridge for breakfast might help you eat less all day. In a series of experiments, researchers in Italy replaced the flour in bread and pasta with oats. They found that even when these foods had identical calorie counts, oat eaters consumed fewer calories over the course of the day.

Banana Shake

Need a Resistant Starch shortcut? Eat a banana. It's the secret reason this shake is such a slimming way to start your morning. If you're not a breakfast eater, shakes are also an easy way to get the Resistant Starch you need without feeling stuffed.

Prep: 5 minutes
Total time: 5 minutes
Makes: 1 serving

Resistant Starch: 4.7g

1 banana
350 ml (12 fl oz) 1% fat milk
2 teaspoons honey
120 ml (4 fl oz) ice

1. Place all ingredients in a blender; process until smooth.

Serving size: 350 ml (12 fl oz) Calories 300; Fat 4g (sat 2.5g, mono 1g, poly 0g); Cholesterol 20mg; Protein 14g; Carbohydrate 57g; Sugars 44g; Fibre 3g; RS 4.7g; Sodium 170mg

Variations:
Banana Shake Plus: Add 2 teaspoons ground flaxseed.
Banana-Cocoa Shake: Add 1 tablespoon unsweetened cocoa powder.
Banana-Berry Shake: Add 25 g (1 oz) berries (any variety).

★CarbStar★
BANANAS
4.7 to 12.5 grams of Resistant Starch per serving, depending on ripeness

Bananas are your richest source of Resistant Starch, with ripe ones offering 4.7 grams of the fat flusher and less ripe (slightly green) bananas containing a whopping 12.5 grams. They are also rich in appetite-suppressing fibre (with 3 grams per 1 medium banana) and contain the amino acid tryptophan, which is converted into the calming brain chemical serotonin to relax and improve your mood.

Big Chopped Salad

You can build this at any salad bar or make it yourself from ingredients you have at home. This salad provides nearly half of your daily fibre, thanks in part to the chickpeas.

Prep: 5 minutes

Total time: 5 minutes

Makes: 1 serving

Resistant Starch: **2.1**g

125 g (4 oz) mixed salad leaves
125 g (4 oz) canned no-salt-added chickpeas, rinsed and drained
100 g (3½ oz) grated carrots
50 g (2 oz) shredded red cabbage
1 tablespoon grated Parmesan cheese
2 tablespoons chopped walnuts
2 tablespoons dried cranberries
2 tablespoons low-fat balsamic vinaigrette

1. Combine first 7 ingredients in a large bowl.

2. Toss with vinaigrette and serve.

Serving size: 400 g (14 oz) Calories 390; Fat 14g (sat 2g, mono 2g, poly 8g); Cholesterol 5mg; Protein 15g; Carbohydrate 60g; Sugars 23g; Fibre 13g; RS 2.1g; Sodium 630mg

Chicken Pitta Sandwich

This easy sandwich will fill you up with lean protein, along with a hearty 5 grams of fibre from the wholemeal pitta and veggies inside. Use pre-cooked chicken strips or rotisserie chicken to save time.

Prep: 5 minutes

Total time: 5 minutes

Makes: 1 serving

40 g (1½ oz) baby spinach
125 g (4 oz) cooked skinless, boneless chicken breast, sliced into 1 cm (½ inch) strips
½ sliced red pepper
2 tablespoons low-fat Italian vinaigrette
1 (15 cm/6 inch) wholemeal pitta, cut in half

1. Combine spinach, chicken, pepper and vinaigrette in a bowl; toss gently.

2. Serve in pitta halves.

Serving size: 2 stuffed pitta halves Calories 400; Fat 10g (sat 1.5g, mono 1.5g, poly 2g); Cholesterol 95mg; Protein 43g; Carbohydrate 36g; Sugars 5g; Fibre 6g; RS 1g; Sodium 670mg

Express Lunch Plate

Grab the ingredients for this fast, filling lunch from the corner deli. This combo is rich in fibre, protein and other metabolism boosters. If you prefer a different type of cheese, swap it.

Prep: 5 minutes

Total time: 5 minutes

Makes: 1 serving

Resistant Starch: 1g

1 large hard-boiled egg
25 g (1 oz) wedge Cheddar cheese
1 apple, cored and sliced
3 rye crackers

1. Arrange all ingredients on a plate and enjoy.

Serving size: 1 plate Calories 400; Fat 15g (sat 8g, mono 5g, poly 1g); Cholesterol 240mg; Protein 16g; Carbohydrate 51g; Sugars 20g; Fibre 9g; RS 1g; Sodium 320mg

Black Bean Tacos

The black beans in this dish should be every dieter's best friend. They provide plenty of Resistant Starch, along with appetite-suppressing fibre and protein. The cheese offers CLA for an extra metabolism kick. To save time, use pre-washed lettuce and ready-grated carrots.

Prep: 5 minutes

Cook: 5 minutes

Total time: 10 minutes

Makes: 2 servings

Resistant Starch: 4.7g

400 g (14 oz) can no-salt-added black beans, rinsed and drained
6 (15 cm/6-inch) corn tortillas
6 tablespoons grated Cheddar cheese
75 g (3 oz) shredded Cos lettuce
175 g (6 oz) grated carrots
60 ml (2 fl oz) salsa

1. Microwave beans at HIGH 2 minutes or until heated through.

2. Heat a nonstick frying pan over medium heat. Add tortillas, one at a time; cook 1 minute on each side.

3. Divide beans evenly between tortillas. Top with even amounts of cheese, lettuce, carrot and salsa.

Serving size: 3 tacos Calories 420; Fat 8g (sat 5g, mono 0.5g, poly 1g); Cholesterol 25mg; Protein 18g; Carbohydrate 69g; Sugars 5g; Fibre 17g; RS 4.7g; Sodium 420mg

★CarbStar★

BEANS

1.5 to 3.8 grams of Resistant Starch per serving

Nearly half of the starch in beans comes from Resistant Starch, making them a powerful weight-loss ally. They are also an incredibly rich source of fibre, providing 15 grams per 250 g (8 oz). It's no wonder that a Canadian study of 1,475 men and women found that those who consumed beans regularly tended to weigh less and have a smaller waist circumference than those who did not eat them. They were also 23 per cent less likely to become overweight over time.

Chicken Pasta Primavera

To save time, batch-cook the pasta and use pre-cooked or rotisserie chicken for this easy, fibre-packed dish. Use a vegetable peeler to make the courgette ribbons.

Prep: 5 minutes
Cook: 15 minutes
Total time: 20 minutes
Makes: 2 servings

Resistant Starch:

2g

50 g (2 oz) uncooked wholewheat pasta spirals
2 teaspoons olive oil
125 g (4 ounces) cooked skinless, boneless chicken breast, sliced into 1 cm (½ in) strips
1 onion, vertically sliced
3 garlic cloves, finely chopped
1 teaspoon dried oregano
⅛ teaspoon salt
⅛ teaspoon pepper
400 g (14 oz) tomatoes, chopped
1 courgette, sliced lengthways into ribbons
2 tablespoons grated Parmesan cheese

1. Cook pasta according to packet directions, omitting salt and fat. Drain.

2. Heat oil in a nonstick frying pan over medium heat. Add chicken; cook 5 minutes.

3. Add onion, garlic, oregano, salt, pepper and tomato to pan; cook 8–10 minutes.

4. Combine chicken mixture, pasta and courgette ribbons; toss gently. Top with Parmesan cheese.

Serving size: 300 g (10 oz) Calories 410; Fat 9g (sat 2g, mono 3.5g, poly 1g); Cholesterol 40mg; Protein 28g; Carbohydrate 61g; Sugars 13g; Fibre 12g; RS 2g; Sodium 480mg

Grilled Burger & Three-Bean Salad

With 29 grams of protein, this is a stick-to-your-ribs meal that – thanks to plenty of metabolism boosters – will fill you up but won't fill you out.

Prep: 5 minutes

Cook: 15 minutes

Total time: 20 minutes

Makes: 2 servings

Resistant Starch:

2.3g

175 g (6 oz) lean minced steak
1 teaspoon olive oil
75 g (3 oz) green beans, fresh or frozen, thawed
125 g (4 oz) canned cannellini beans, rinsed and drained
125 g (4 oz) canned kidney beans, rinsed and drained
100 g (3½ oz) carrot, peeled and chopped
½ green pepper, chopped
40 g (1½ oz) wholemeal hamburger buns
2 tablespoons low-fat Italian vinaigrette
Cos lettuce leaves
4 tomato slices

1. Divide beef into 2 equal portions, shaping each into a 1 cm (½-inch) thick patty.

2. Heat oil in a nonstick frying pan over medium heat. Place patties in pan; cook 6 minutes each side or until a meat thermometer inserted into middle of burger reads 71°C (160°F).

3. Combine green beans, cannellini beans, kidney beans, carrot, pepper and vinaigrette in a bowl; toss gently.

4. On the bottom of each bun, place a few lettuce leaves and 2 slices tomato; top with burger and other half of bun. Serve bean salad alongside burgers.

Serving size: 1 burger and 200 g (7 oz) salad
Calories 400; Fat 11g (sat 2g, mono 4g, poly 2g); Cholesterol 45mg; Protein 29g; Carbohydrate 50g; Sugars 9g; Fibre 12g; RS 2.3g; Sodium 580mg

Prawn Stir-Fry with Ginger

To save time, use a fast-cooking brown rice to get this crowd-pleasing meal on the table even faster.

Prep: 5 minutes

Cook: 10 minutes

Total time: 15 minutes

Makes: 2 servings

Resistant Starch: 2.6g

2 teaspoons dark sesame oil
2 tablespoons less-sodium soy sauce
1 tablespoon honey
1 tablespoon grated peeled fresh ginger
2 garlic cloves, finely chopped
400 g (14 oz) frozen stir-fry vegetables, thawed
75 g (3 oz) (about 14 medium) frozen cooked prawns, thawed
300 g (10 oz) cooked brown rice
2 tablespoons flaked almonds
1 spring onion, chopped

1. Heat oil in a large nonstick frying pan over medium heat. Add soy sauce, honey, ginger and garlic; cook 1 minute.

2. Add vegetables, prawns and cooked rice; cook 8 minutes.

3. Remove from heat. Top with almonds and spring onion.

Serving size: 400 g (14 oz) Calories 410; Fat 9g (sat 1.5g, mono 4g, poly 3.5g); Cholesterol 65mg; Protein 17g; Carbohydrate 61g; Sugars 14g; Fibre 6g; RS 2.6g; Sodium 710mg

Griddled Salmon & Potatoes

Salmon, like tuna, is packed with metabolism-boosting omega-3 fatty acids. This dish also features CLA in the cheese, Resistant Starch from the potatoes and fibre from the leaves.

Prep: 8 minutes
Cook: 12 minutes
Total time: 20 minutes
Makes: 2 servings

Resistant Starch: **2.1** g

1 (175 g/6 oz) salmon fillet (about 2.5 cm/1 inch thick)
Cooking spray
2 medium potatoes
Salt and pepper, to taste
4 tablespoons grated Parmesan cheese
75 g (3 oz) mixed salad leaves
200 g (7 oz) tomatoes, chopped
2 tablespoons low-fat balsamic vinaigrette
1 lemon

1. Heat a nonstick frying pan or griddle over medium-high heat. Coat fish with cooking spray. Add fish to pan, and cook 6 minutes on each side or until fish flakes easily when tested with a fork.

2. While fish cooks, pierce potatoes with a fork; arrange in a circle on kitchen paper in a microwave oven. Microwave at HIGH 8–10 minutes, turning potatoes after 5 minutes. Let stand 5 minutes.

3. Cut the cooked potatoes in half, and sprinkle with the salt, pepper and Parmesan cheese.

4. Combine salad leaves, tomatoes and vinaigrette in a bowl; toss gently.

5. Cut lemon in half, and squeeze lemon juice over fish. Serve salmon with potatoes and salad.

Serving size: 75 g (3 oz) salmon, 2 potato halves and 150 g (5 oz) salad Calories 410; Fat 12g (sat 3g, mono 2g, poly 2g); Cholesterol 50mg; Protein 30g; Carbohydrate 49g; Sugars 7g; Fibre 7g; RS 2.1g; Sodium 660mg

★CarbStar★
POTATOES
1 to 3.7 grams of Resistant Starch

In addition to fibre and Resistant Starch, potatoes are a natural source of a proteinase inhibitor, a natural chemical that boosts satiety hormones and curbs appetite. Potatoes are also incredibly filling and – at 300 calories for a large, baked spud – great for weight loss.

Kickstart Snacks

During Phase 1, you can choose one snack a day.
Try one of these:

- **Cannellini & Herb Hummus with Crudités** (shown at right)

- **Potato crisps:** Crunch on 24 crisps (about 25 g/1 oz).

- **Black Beans & Chips:** Enjoy 2 tablespoons canned black beans, rinsed and drained, with 8 corn tortilla chips.

- **Trail Mix:** Combine 15 g (½ oz) cornflakes, 2 tablespoons flaked almonds and 2 tablespoons dried cherries.

- **Greek Yogurt Parfait:** Top 175 g (6 oz) natural low-fat Greek yogurt with 2 teaspoons honey and 2 tablespoons rolled oats, uncooked or toasted.

- **Almond Butter Crackers:** Nosh on 2 teaspoons almond butter spread on 2 rye crackers.

Cannellini & Herb Hummus with Crudités

The MUFAs, fibre, and Resistant Starch in this snack will tide you over until your next meal.

Prep: 5 minutes

Total time: 5 minutes

Makes: 1 serving

Resistant Starch: 2g

65 g (2½ oz) canned cannellini beans, rinsed and drained
1 tablespoon chopped chives
1 tablespoon lemon juice
2 teaspoons olive oil
75 g (3 oz) assorted raw vegetables, such as chopped broccoli florets, cherry tomatoes, courgette batons, and sugar snap peas

1. Combine beans, chives, lemon juice and oil in a small bowl. Mash with a fork until mixture thickens but still has texture.

2. Serve with raw vegetables.

Serving size: 60 ml (2 fl oz) hummus and 75 g (3 oz) raw vegetables Calories 150; Fat 10g (sat 1.5g, mono 7g, poly 1g); Cholesterol 0mg; Protein 4g; Carbohydrate 14g; Sugars 3g; Fibre 3g; RS 2g; Sodium 35mg

21-DAY IMMERSION RECIPES

Apple & Almond Muesli

If mornings are hectic for you, make this dish the day before. Mix all of the ingredients, cover and refrigerate overnight.

Prep: 5 minutes
Stand: 7 minutes
Total time: 12 minutes
Makes: 1 serving

Resistant Starch:
4.6g

50 g (2 oz) rolled oats
120 ml (4 fl oz) 1% fat milk
1 apple, cored and chopped
2 tablespoons flaked almonds
2 teaspoons honey

1. Combine oats and milk in a small bowl; let stand 7 minutes.

2. Stir in apple, almonds and honey.

Serving size: 500 ml (16 fl oz) Calories 400; Fat 10g (sat 2g, mono 5g, poly 2.5g); Cholesterol 5mg; Protein 12g; Carbohydrate 72g; Sugars 38g; Fibre 10g; RS 4.6g; Sodium 55mg

Banana Yogurt Parfait with Maple Oat Topping

Uncooked oats offer four times as much Resistant Starch as cooked, which is why this recipe calls for you to only lightly toast them.

Prep: 5 minutes

Cook: 5 minutes

Total time: 10 minutes

Makes: 1 serving

Resistant Starch:
8.2g

6 tablespoons rolled oats
1 tablespoon pure maple syrup
180 ml (6 fl oz) natural low-fat Greek yogurt
1 banana, sliced

1. Heat a nonstick frying pan over medium heat. In a small bowl, combine oats and maple syrup; add oat mixture to pan, and cook 2–3 minutes.

2. Place yogurt in a bowl and top with banana and toasted oats.

Serving size: 350 ml (12 fl oz) Calories 380; Fat 6g (sat 3g, mono 1g, poly 1g); Cholesterol 10mg; Protein 19g; Carbohydrate 67g; Sugars 34g; Fibre 6g; RS 8.2g; Sodium 60mg

Breakfast Barley with Banana & Sunflower Seeds

With a whopping 7.6 grams of Resistant Starch plus some metabolism-boosting fibre and MUFAs, to boot, this is an ultrasatisfying morning meal.

Prep: 5 minutes
Cook: 10 minutes
Total time: 15 minutes
Makes: 1 serving

Resistant Starch:

7.6g

150 ml (5 fl oz) water
75 g (3 oz) uncooked quick-cooking pearl barley
1 banana, sliced
1 teaspoon honey
1 tablespoon unsalted sunflower seeds

1. Combine water and barley in a small microwave-safe bowl. Microwave at HIGH 6 minutes.

2. Stir and let stand 2 minutes.

3. Top with banana slices, honey and sunflower seeds.

Serving size: 240 ml (8 fl oz) Calories 410; Fat 6g (sat 0.5g, mono 2g, poly 2.5g); Cholesterol 0mg; Protein 10g; Carbohydrate 86g; Sugars 21g; Fibre 14g; RS 7.6g; Sodium 15mg

Blueberry Oat Pancakes with Maple Yogurt

Because this dish takes some time to prepare, save it for a weekend morning when you're not in a rush. You can substitute natural low-fat yogurt for the Greek yogurt. You can use either fresh or thawed frozen unsweetened berries.

Prep: 5 minutes

Cook: 10 minutes

Total time: 15 minutes

Makes: 2 servings

100 g (3½ oz) **rolled oats**
125 g (4 oz) **low-fat cottage cheese**
2 large **eggs**
1 teaspoon **vanilla extract**
125 g (4 oz) **blueberries**
Cooking spray
180 ml (6 fl oz) **natural low-fat Greek yogurt**
1 tablespoon **maple syrup**

1. Combine oats, cottage cheese, eggs and vanilla in a blender or food processor; process until smooth. Gently stir in the blueberries.

2. Heat a large nonstick frying pan over medium heat. Coat pan with cooking spray. Spoon about 2 tablespoons batter per pancake into pan. Cook 3 minutes or until tops are covered with bubbles and edges look cooked. Carefully turn pancakes over, and cook 3 more minutes or until golden.

3. Combine yogurt and maple syrup; serve alongside pancakes.

Serving size: 3 (7.5 cm/3 inch) pancakes and about 120 ml (4 fl oz) yogurt mixture Calories 410; Fat 12g (sat 3.5g, mono 3g, poly 2g); Cholesterol 220mg; Protein 26g; Carbohydrate 50g; Sugars 20g; Fibre 6g; RS 4.6g; Sodium 330mg

Broccoli & Feta Omelette with Toast

Who needs breakfast at a café when you can whip up a dish like this in no time flat? Use either fresh or frozen broccoli – both work just fine. The feta cheese adds some CLA plus a punch of flavour, too.

Prep: 5 minutes
Cook: 10 minutes
Total time: 15 minutes
Makes: 1 serving

Resistant Starch:
1.8g

Cooking spray
175 g (6 oz) broccoli, chopped
2 large eggs, whisked
2 tablespoons crumbled Feta cheese
¼ teaspoon dried dill
2 slices rye bread, toasted

1. Heat a nonstick frying pan over medium heat. Coat pan with cooking spray. Add broccoli, and cook 3 minutes.

2. Combine eggs, feta and dill in a small bowl. Add egg mixture to pan. Cook 3–4 minutes; fold in half with a spatula and cook 2 more minutes or until cooked through. Serve with toast.

Serving size: 1 omelette and 2 pieces toast Calories 390; Fat 19g (sat 6g, mono 5g, poly 2g); Cholesterol 440mg; Protein 23g; Carbohydrate 35g; Sugars 5g; Fibre 6g; RS 1.8g; Sodium 550mg

Cherry-Ginger Scones

Bet you never thought you'd be eating scones while you were on a diet! These scones, however, are so diet friendly that they aren't even a dessert – you can have them for breakfast. High in fibre, protein and Resistant Starch, they will keep you satisfied in every way.

Prep: 20 minutes

Bake: 25 minutes

Total time: 45 minutes

Makes: 8 servings

Resistant Starch:

1.2g

250 g (8 oz) wholemeal flour
100 g (3½ oz) rolled oats
50 g (2 oz) brown sugar
2 teaspoons baking powder
½ teaspoon bicarbonate of soda
¼ teaspoon salt
125 g (4 oz) unsalted butter
150 g (5 oz) dried cherries
75 g (3 oz) crystallized ginger, coarsely chopped
60 ml (2 fl oz) low-fat buttermilk
2 large egg whites, whisked
Plain flour (as needed)

1. Preheat oven to 180°C/350°F/gas mark 4. Line a baking sheet with baking parchment, and set aside.

2. Combine flour, oats, brown sugar, baking powder, bicarbonate of soda, and salt in a food processor. Process 10 seconds or until oats are finely chopped. Add butter; process until mixture resembles coarse breadcrumbs.

3. Transfer flour mixture to a large mixing bowl; stir in cherries and crystallized ginger.

4. Combine buttermilk and egg whites in a small bowl; stir with a whisk. Add buttermilk mixture to flour mixture; stir just until a sticky dough forms.

5. Transfer dough to a prepared baking sheet, and pat into a 23 cm (9 inch) circle (about 2.5 cm/1 inch thick). Sprinkle with plain flour, if necessary, to keep the dough from sticking to hands. Divide the dough into 8 equal wedges. Separate wedges slightly, and bake in preheated oven for 25 minutes or until golden brown and a skewer inserted in centre comes out clean.

Serving size: 1 scone Calories 348; Fat 13g (sat 7.5g, mono 3g, poly 1g); Cholesterol 31mg; Protein 6g; Carbohydrate 53g; Sugars 20g; Fibre 5g; RS 1.2g; Sodium 271mg

Coconut French Toast with Raspberry Syrup

Save this delicious dish for a weekend morning when you are not in a rush. You can use fresh or thawed frozen unsweetened raspberries.

Prep: 5 minutes
Cook: 10 minutes
Total time: 15 minutes
Makes: 2 servings

Resistant Starch:

1.2g

2 large eggs
120 ml (4 fl oz) 1% fat milk
1 teaspoon vanilla extract
4 (1 cm/½ inch-thick) slices sourdough bread
2 tablespoons dessicated coconut
Cooking spray
125 g (4 oz) raspberries
2 tablespoons pure maple syrup

1. In a large bowl, whisk together eggs, milk and vanilla.

2. Lightly dip bread slices in egg mixture; pat dessicated coconut onto both sides of bread.

3. Heat a large nonstick frying pan over medium heat. Coat pan with cooking spray. Add bread slices; cook 4 minutes on each side or until golden.

4. Combine raspberries and maple syrup in a small microwave-safe bowl. Microwave at HIGH 30 seconds. Serve over French toast.

Serving size: 2 pieces French toast and 4 tablespoons syrup Calories 410; Fat 12g (sat 5g, mono 2.5g, poly 1.5g); Cholesterol 215mg; Protein 16g; Carbohydrate 58g; Sugars 20g; Fibre 6g; RS 1.2g; Sodium 470mg

Cornflakes, Low-Fat Milk & Berries

It doesn't matter what types of berries you use for this recipe. All of them – strawberries, blueberries, raspberries, blackberries – are high in fibre, low in calories and rich in antioxidants.

Prep: 5 minutes
Total time: 5 minutes
Makes: 1 serving

Resistant Starch:
1.8g

50 g (2 oz) cornflakes
240 ml (8 fl oz) 1% fat milk
125 g (4 oz) berries, fresh or frozen, thawed

1. Place cornflakes in a small bowl. Top with milk and berries.

Serving size: 750 ml (1 ¼ pints) Calories 370; Fat 3g (sat 1.5g, mono 1g, poly 0g), Cholesterol 10mg; Protein 13g, Carbohydrate 78g; Sugars 27g; Fibre 6g; RS 1.8g; Sodium 640mg

Porridge with Prune & Banana Compote

A rich source of vitamin C and polyphenols (a type of antioxidant thought to protect brain cells from damage), dried plums – prunes – add rich flavour to this traditional morning dish.

Prep: 5 minutes

Cook: 5 minutes

Total time: 10 minutes

Makes: 1 serving

Resistant Starch: 5.2g

240 ml (8 fl oz) 1% fat milk
50 g (2 oz) rolled oats
3 dried prunes, chopped
1 banana, diced
1 tablespoon crystallized ginger, chopped

1. Combine milk and oats in a small microwave-safe bowl. Microwave at HIGH 3–5 minutes.

2. Combine prunes, banana and crystallized ginger; sprinkle over porridge.

Serving size: 350 ml (12 fl oz) Calories 420; Fat 6g (sat 2g, mono 1.5g, poly 1g); Cholesterol 10mg; Protein 15g; Carbohydrate 83g; Sugars 35g; Fibre 8g; RS 5.2g; Sodium 115mg

Toast with Walnut & Pear Breakfast Spread

Cottage cheese packs CLA, walnuts add some omega-3s, and pear contributes fibre, making this easy dish a great way to jump-start your metabolism in the morning.

Prep: 5 minutes
Total time: 5 minutes
Makes: 1 serving

125 g (4 oz) low-fat, low-sodium cottage cheese
1 pear, chopped
1 tablespoon chopped walnuts
2 slices sourdough bread, toasted

1. Place cottage cheese in a blender or food processor; process until smooth. Transfer to a small bowl.

2. Stir pear and walnuts into cottage cheese.

3. Spread cottage cheese mixture on toast.

Serving size: 2 pieces toast; 240 ml (8 fl oz) spread Calories 400; Fat 7g (sat 1g, mono 1g, poly 4g); Cholesterol 5mg; Protein 22g; Carbohydrate 64g; Sugars 22g; Fibre 7g; RS 1.2g; Sodium 390mg

Polenta Fritters with Asparagus & Eggs

Asparagus is one of those vegetables that tastes wonderful when it is in season in spring, but not so much when it's out of season. During the autumn and winter months, use frozen asparagus or substitute broccoli florets or spinach.

Prep: 5 minutes
Cook: 10 minutes
Total time: 15 minutes
Makes: 1 serving

Resistant Starch: 1.5g

Cooking spray
175 g (6 oz) ready-to-use polenta, cut into
    4 (1 cm/½-inch thick) slices
6 asparagus spears, trimmed
2 large eggs
2 tablespoons grated Parmesan cheese
Black pepper, to taste

1. Heat a large nonstick frying pan over medium heat. Coat pan with cooking spray. Add polenta and asparagus; cook 8 minutes, turning once.

2. Push polenta and asparagus to side of pan. Recoat pan with cooking spray. Add eggs, and fry until yolks are set, about 3 minutes.

3. Serve eggs on warm polenta with asparagus on the side. Sprinkle with cheese and black pepper.

Serving size: 4 pieces polenta, 2 eggs and 6 asparagus spears Calories 380; Fat 17g (sat 5g, mono 4g, poly 1.5g); Cholesterol 433mg; Protein 23g; Carbohydrate 30g; Sugars 6g; Fibre 4g; RS 1.5g; Sodium 600mg

★CarbStar★
POLENTA
1 gram of Resistant Starch per 8 tablespoons cooked

This soft, creamy grain is made from cooked cornmeal. Naturally high in Resistant Starch, polenta is also rich in fibre and contains a decent amount of protein, too. And it's versatile. It can be cooked into a creamy consistency or baked into crunchy sticks. In fact, you can even use it instead of white bread to make croutons.

Potato-Crusted Spinach Quiche

Usually quiche pastry is made from butter and flour. This version uses grated potatoes, which cuts fat and calories and ups the amount of Resistant Starch.

Prep: 20 minutes

Cook: 1 hour

Total time: 1 hour 20 minutes

Makes: 4 servings

Resistant Starch: 1.4g

1 tablespoon olive oil, divided
600 g (1 lb 4 oz) potatoes, grated
1 large egg white, whisked
1 tablespoon plain flour
½ teaspoon salt
175 g (6 oz) fresh spinach
½ medium onion, chopped
2 tablespoons water
6 large eggs
50 g (2 oz) low-fat ricotta cheese
¼ teaspoon freshly ground black pepper
50 g (2 oz) Gruyère cheese, grated
25 g (1 oz) back bacon, finely chopped

1. Preheat oven to 200°C/400°F/gas mark 6. Coat inside of a 23 cm (9 inch) deep pie dish with 1 teaspoon olive oil; set aside.

2. Combine potatoes and egg white in a large bowl; toss lightly. Add flour and salt; toss to coat. Transfer to pie dish, and pat evenly into bottom and sides to form case. Drizzle remaining 2 teaspoons oil over case. Bake in preheated oven for 15 minutes or until edges begin to brown. Remove from oven. Reduce oven temperature to 180°/350°/gas mark 4.

3. While case bakes, place spinach, onion and 2 tablespoons water in a microwave-safe bowl. Microwave at HIGH 2 minutes or until spinach begins to wilt; drain. Place spinach mixture in a colander, and squeeze to drain; coarsely chop, and set aside.

4. Combine eggs and ricotta cheese in a large mixing bowl; stir with a whisk until smooth. Add black pepper. Stir in spinach mixture, half the cheese and the bacon.

5. Pour egg mixture over potato case; spread with the back of a spoon to distribute evenly, leaving a 1 cm (½ inch) rim along the outer edge. Sprinkle remaining Gruyère on top. Bake for 50–55 minutes, until puffed and golden. Cool on a wire rack 10–15 minutes before serving. Slice into 4 equal pieces and serve.

Serving size: ¼ **of quiche** Calories 380; Fat 17g (sat 6g, mono 7g, poly 2g); Cholesterol 340mg; Protein 20g; Carbohydrate 37g; Sugars 1g; Fibre 6g; RS 1.4g; Sodium 720mg

Cheddar & Egg on Rye

The protein and fibre in this easy dish will keep you satisfied all morning. If you don't like Cheddar, substitute any hard cheese.

Prep: 5 minutes

Cook: 5 minutes

Total time: 10 minutes

Makes: 1 serving

Resistant Starch:

1.8g

Cooking spray
1 large egg
2 slices rye bread, toasted
1 slice mature Cheddar cheese
1 small apple, cored and sliced

1. Heat a nonstick frying pan over medium heat. Coat pan with cooking spray. Add egg; cook until set, about 3 minutes.

2. Top toast with cheese; place egg over cheese. Serve with apple slices on the side.

Serving size: 1 sandwich and 1 apple Calories 420; Fat 18g (sat 8g, mono 5g, poly 1.5g); Cholesterol 240mg; Protein 19g; Carbohydrate 49g; Sugars 18g; Fibre 7g; RS 1.8g; Sodium 620mg

★CarbStar★

RYE, PUMPERNICKEL, OR SOURDOUGH BREAD

0.6 to 1.3 grams of Resistant Starch per slice

Bread made from rye, pumpernickel or sourdough is rich in Resistant Starch and fibre. One Swedish study found that rye bread decreased hunger more than wholemeal bread.

Tomato & Mozzarella Melt

This is a great breakfast idea if you prefer savoury morning fare. Think of it as a mini pizza!

Prep: 5 minutes
Cook: 5 minutes
Total time: 10 minutes
Makes: 1 serving

Resistant Starch: 1.8g

2 slices rye bread
8 fresh basil leaves
4 tomato slices
2 (25 g/1 oz) slices low-fat mozzarella
1 orange, cut into wedges

1. Top each bread slice with 4 basil leaves, 2 tomato slices and 1 slice cheese.

2. Melt the open sandwiches under a grill for 4–5 minutes or until cheese is bubbling. Serve with orange wedges.

Serving size: 2 pieces topped toast and 1 orange
Calories 370; Fat 11g (sat 6g, mono 3.5g, poly 1g); Cholesterol 35mg; Protein 21g; Carbohydrate 48g; Sugars 17g; Fibre 7g; RS 1.8g; Sodium 730mg

Courgette & Potato Scramble with Bacon

You'll be amazed how much turkey bacon tastes like the real thing for a fraction of the fat and calories. To save time on this dish, use shop-bought grated potatoes.

Prep: 10 minutes
Cook: 15 minutes
Total time: 25 minutes
Makes: 1 serving

Resistant Starch: 1.4g

1 small potato, grated (or 125 g/4 oz ready-grated potato)
½ courgette, diced
½ teaspoon dried oregano
⅛ teaspoon salt
⅛ teaspoon pepper
Cooking spray
2 large eggs, whisked
Salt and pepper, to taste (optional)
2 rashers cooked turkey bacon

1. Squeeze grated potato dry with kitchen paper. Combine potato, courgette, oregano, salt and pepper.

2. Heat a large nonstick frying pan over medium heat. Coat pan with cooking spray. Add potato mix, and cook 10 minutes, stirring once, until tender and lightly golden. Add eggs, and cook 3–4 minutes or until eggs are set. Season to taste, and serve with bacon.

Serving size: 500 ml (16 fl oz) scramble and 2 slices turkey bacon Calories 370; Fat 19g (sat 4.5g, mono 6g, poly 3g); Cholesterol 450mg; Protein 21g; Carbohydrate 32g; Sugars 5g; Fibre 5g; RS 1.4g; Sodium 504mg

Rocket Salad
with Lemon-Dijon Dressing

Most croutons are made from stale white bread, which has hardly any Resistant Starch or fibre. Here, you'll use rye bread for an extra dose of Resistant Starch.

Prep: 7 minutes

Total time: 7 minutes

Makes: 1 serving

Resistant Starch: 1.8g

1 tablespoon lemon juice
1 teaspoon olive oil
1 teaspoon Dijon mustard
125 g (4 oz) rocket
125 g (4 oz) cherry tomatoes
125 g (4 oz) canned cannellini beans, rinsed and drained
2 slices rye bread, toasted and cut into 2.5 cm (1 inch) cubes
1 tablespoon grated Parmesan cheese

1. Combine first 3 ingredients in a small bowl, stirring with a whisk.

2. Combine rocket, tomatoes and beans in a large bowl. Add dressing; toss gently.

3. Top with rye bread croutons and cheese.

Serving size: 350 g (12 oz) Calories 400; Fat 10g (sat 2g, mono 4g, poly 1.5g); Cholesterol 5mg; Protein 18g; Carbohydrate 61g; Sugars 7g; Fibre 11g; RS 1.8g; Sodium 710mg

Black Bean & Courgette Quesadillas

If you're making this lunch ahead and taking it to the office, just pop it in the microwave for 1 minute to reheat it.

Prep: 5 minutes

Cook: 2 minutes

Total time: 7 minutes

Makes: 1 serving

Resistant Starch:

4.7g

125 g (4 oz) canned black beans, rinsed and drained
2 tablespoons salsa
1 courgette, finely chopped
4 (15 cm/6 inch) corn tortillas
4 tablespoons grated Cheddar cheese

1. Combine beans and salsa in a small bowl; mash with a fork. Stir in courgettes.

2. Layer 2 tortillas with half of the bean mixture, sprinkle with 2 tablespoons cheese, and top with remaining 2 tortillas. Repeat with remaining tortillas, bean mixture and cheese.

3. Cook quesadillas under the grill for 1 minute on each side until cheese is melted and bubbly.

Serving size: 2 quesadillas Calories 400; Fat 11g (sat 6g, mono 0.5g, poly 1.5g); Cholesterol 30mg; Protein 18g; Carbohydrate 65g; Sugars 4g; Fibre 13g; RS 4.7g; Sodium 670mg

Curried Egg Salad Sandwich

The curry adds a health-promoting antioxidant jolt to this traditional comfort dish. To save prep time, batch-cook a dozen eggs at the beginning of each week so you always have some handy.

Prep: 7 minutes

Total time: 7 minutes

Makes: 1 serving

Resistant Starch: 1.8g

2 hard-boiled eggs, chopped
2 tablespoons natural low-fat Greek yogurt
2 tablespoons chopped red pepper
¼ teaspoon curry powder
Dash of salt
⅛ teaspoon pepper
2 slices rye bread, toasted
25 g (1 oz) fresh spinach
1 orange, sliced

1. Combine eggs, yogurt, red pepper, curry powder, salt and pepper in a small bowl; stir well.

2. Place spinach on 1 slice of bread, and top with egg salad. Place other piece of bread on top. Slice in half on the diagonal with a sharp knife. Serve with orange slices.

Serving size: 1 sandwich and 1 orange Calories 414; Fat 14g (sat 4g, mono 5g, poly 2g); Cholesterol 426mg; Protein 22g; Carbohydrate 51g; Sugars 18g; Fibre 8g; RS 1.8g; Sodium 654mg

Greek Lentil Soup with Toasted Pitta

Lentils are a great source of Resistant Starch and fibre. Double or triple this recipe, and freeze leftovers in individual containers.

Prep: 10 minutes

Cook: 20 minutes

Total time: 30 minutes

Makes: 4 servings

Resistant Starch:

5.3g

1 tablespoon olive oil
2 celery stalks, chopped
2 carrots, peeled and chopped
1 onion, chopped
2 garlic cloves, finely chopped
2 teaspoons dried oregano
½ teaspoon salt
½ teaspoon pepper
2 litres (3½ pints) water
200 g (7 oz) dried lentils
2 tablespoons fresh lemon juice (about 1 lemon)
4 wholemeal pittas, each cut into 4 triangles and toasted

1. Heat oil in a large saucepan over medium heat. Add celery, carrot, onion, garlic, oregano, salt and pepper; cook 5 minutes.

2. Add the water and lentils. Simmer, partially covered, 15 minutes.

3. With a stick blender or potato masher, purée soup until semi-smooth and thick.

4. Drizzle with lemon juice; serve with toasted pitta.

Serving size: 500 ml (16 fl oz) soup and 1 pitta
Calories 370; Fat 6g (sat 0.5g, mono 2.5g, poly 1.5g); Cholesterol 0mg; Protein 19g; Carbohydrate 65g; Sugars 6g; Fibre 21g; RS 5.3g; Sodium 680mg

Ham, Sliced Pear & Cheese Sandwich

The pear adds flavour, texture and fibre to this traditional ham-and-cheese sandwich.

Prep: 10 minutes

Total time: 10 minutes

Makes: 1 serving

Resistant Starch:

2.6g

1 tablespoon natural low-fat Greek yogurt
¼ teaspoon dried dill
2 slices pumpernickel bread
1 (25g/1 oz) slice lean ham
1 small pear, thinly sliced
1 (25g/1 oz) slice low-sodium Gruyère or Emmental cheese

1. Combine yogurt and dill in a small bowl; stir until blended.

2. Spread yogurt mixture on 1 slice of bread. Top with ham, half of the pear slices, cheese and remaining bread slice. Slice in half using a sharp knife. Serve with remaining pear slices on the side.

Serving size: 1 sandwich and 1 pear Calories 410; Fat 13g (sat 6g, mono 4g, poly 1g); Cholesterol 43mg; Protein 22g; Carbohydrate 55g; Sugars 16g; Fibre 9g; RS 2.6g; Sodium 710mg

Indian Chicken Salad with Peanuts

If you are short on time, use pre-cooked white meat chicken strips or rotisserie chicken and bottled light sesame-ginger dressing for this recipe.

Prep: 10 minutes

Cook: 5 minutes

Total time: 15 minutes

Makes: 1 serving

Resistant Starch:

2g

1 potato, cut into 1 cm (½ inch) cubes
Cooking spray
⅛ teaspoon salt
⅛ teaspoon pepper
2 tablespoons water
2 tablespoons lime juice
1 teaspoon dark sesame oil
1 teaspoon honey
1 teaspoon grated peeled fresh ginger
125 g (4 oz) chopped Cos lettuce
50 g (2 oz) grilled or baked skinless chicken, chopped
2 tablespoons chopped peanuts
1 tablespoon chopped fresh mint
1 tablespoon chopped fresh coriander

1. Place potato in a microwave-safe dish. Spray potato with cooking spray, and sprinkle with salt and pepper. Add 2 tablespoons water; cover and microwave at HIGH 5 minutes or until tender.

2. Combine lime juice, oil, honey and ginger in a small bowl; stir well with a whisk.

3. Combine potato, lettuce, chicken, peanuts, mint and coriander in a large bowl. Add dressing; toss gently to coat.

Serving size: 350 g (12 oz) Calories 420; Fat 17g (sat 2.5g, mono 7g, poly 6g); Cholesterol 50mg; Protein 27g; Carbohydrate 44g; Sugars 10g; Fibre 8g; RS 2g; Sodium 360mg

Mediterranean Pasta Salad

Peas are an easy way to bump up the Resistant Starch in any dish. Just keep a bag of frozen peas in the freezer so you can easily add them to this and other grain salads.

Prep: 15 minutes

Cook: 15 minutes

Total time: 30 minutes

Makes: 4 servings

Resistant Starch: **2.4**g

125 g (4 oz) uncooked wholewheat farfalle (bow tie pasta)
1 teaspoon lemon zest
2 tablespoons lemon juice
2 teaspoons olive oil
400 g (14 fl oz) can artichoke hearts in water, drained and chopped
125 g (4 oz) fresh low-fat mozzarella cheese, cubed
4 tablespoons chopped bottled roasted red peppers
4 tablespoons chopped fresh parsley
75 g (3 oz) frozen peas

1. Cook pasta according to packet instructions, omitting salt and fat.

2. While pasta cooks, combine zest and juice of 1 lemon and 2 teaspoons olive oil in a large bowl; stir well with a whisk. Add artichoke hearts, cheese, red pepper and parsley; toss to combine.

3. Place the peas in a colander; when the pasta is cooked, drain pasta over peas. Shake well to drain, but do not run under cold water. Add the pasta and peas to the artichoke mixture, and toss well until thoroughly combined. Serve warm or at room temperature.

Serving size: 175 g (6 oz) Calories 418; Fat 16g (sat 8g, mono 2g, poly 1g); Cholesterol 45mg; Protein 20g; Carbohydrate 50g; Sugars 3g; Fibre 8g; RS 2.4g; Sodium 196mg

Middle Eastern Rice Salad

The dates in this recipe provide plenty of appetite-suppressing fibre, while the brown rice and chickpeas pack more than 4 grams of Resistant Starch per serving.

Prep: 15 minutes

Cook: 5 minutes

Total time: 20 minutes

Makes: 4 servings

Resistant Starch: **4.1**g

2 tablespoons olive oil
½ red onion, thinly sliced
480 ml (16 oz) can chickpeas, rinsed and drained
½ teaspoon ground cumin
¼ teaspoon salt
Freshly ground black pepper, to taste
600 g (1 lb 4 oz) cooked brown rice
75 g (3 oz) chopped dates
4 tablespoons chopped fresh mint
4 tablespoons chopped fresh parsley

1. Heat oil in a large nonstick frying pan over medium-high heat. Add onion, and cook, stirring often, 5 minutes or until onion begins to brown. Remove from heat, and stir in chickpeas, cumin and salt. Season to taste with freshly ground black pepper.

2. Combine rice, chickpea mixture, dates, mint and parsley in a large bowl. Toss well until thoroughly combined. Serve warm or at room temperature.

Serving size: 300 g (10 oz) Calories 380; Fat 9g (sat 1g, mono 5.5g, poly 1g); Cholesterol 0mg; Protein 8g; Carbohydrate 67g; Sugars 18g; Fibre 8g; RS 4.1g; Sodium 360mg

★CarbStar★
BROWN RICE
1.7 grams of Resistant Starch per 100 g (3½ oz)

Brown rice may cook more slowly than its refined white cousins, but it digests more slowly, too. One study found that blood sugar levels were 24 per cent lower in people who consumed brown rice, compared with participants in a control group. Another study found that eating a black and brown rice mix is healthier than eating white rice; it resulted in a greater reduction in weight, body mass index and body fat.

Moroccan Chicken Pitta

This quick-and-easy lunch option can be made even easier if you use pre-cooked chicken strips or rotisserie chicken.

Prep: 10 minutes

Total time: 10 minutes

Makes: 1 serving

Resistant Starch:

1g

4 tablespoons natural low-fat Greek yogurt
½ teaspoon honey
⅛ teaspoon salt
⅛ teaspoon ground cumin
⅛ teaspoon ground cinnamon
75 g (3 oz) grilled or baked chicken, chopped
100 g (3½ oz) grated carrot
2 tablespoons chopped dates
1 wholemeal pitta, halved
25 g (1 oz) fresh spinach

1. Combine first 5 ingredients in a small bowl, stirring well with a whisk.

2. Combine chicken, carrot and dates in a bowl. Add dressing; toss gently to coat.

3. Fill pitta halves with chicken mixture and spinach.

Serving size: 2 stuffed pitta halves Calories 420; Fat 6g (sat 1.5, mono 1g, poly 1.5g); Cholesterol 75mg; Protein 39g; Carbohydrate 56g; Sugars 24g; Fibre 8g; RS 1g; Sodium 750mg

Pecan-Crusted Goat's Cheese Salad with Pomegranate Vinaigrette

Rich in MUFAs, CLA, fibre and oleic acid, this just might win the award for the most filling, slimming and satisfying salad ever created.

Prep: 5 minutes

Cook: 10 minutes

Total time: 15 minutes

Makes: 1 serving

Resistant Starch:

1g

125 g (4 oz) ready-to-use polenta, cut into 2.5 cm (1 inch) cubes
Cooking spray
25 g (1 oz) goat's cheese
1 tablespoon chopped pecans
2 tablespoons pomegranate juice
1 teaspoon olive oil
1 teaspoon Dijon mustard
150 g (5 oz) fresh spinach
100 g (3½ oz) grated carrot

1. Heat a large nonstick frying pan over medium heat. Coat polenta cubes with cooking spray. Add to pan, and cook 5 minutes. Turn croutons; cook 5 minutes more or until golden.

2. Shape goat's cheese into a patty; coat with chopped pecans.

3. Combine juice, oil and mustard in a small bowl; stir well with a whisk.

4. Arrange spinach and carrot on a plate. Top with polenta cubes, pecan-crusted cheese and dressing.

Serving size: 400 g (14 oz) Calories 370; Fat 21g (sat 7g, mono 8g, poly 2g); Cholesterol 20mg; Protein 11g; Carbohydrate 36g; Sugars 10g; Fibre 7g; RS 1g; Sodium 720mg

Pesto Turkey Club

Pesto packs two metabolism boosters – olive oil and pine nuts. Add that to the pumpernickel bread (Resistant Starch), apple (fibre) and turkey (protein), and you've got an ultra-slimming club sandwich.

Prep: 5 minutes
Total time: 5 minutes
Makes: 1 serving

Resistant Starch:
2.6g

2 teaspoons prepared pesto
2 slices pumpernickel bread
25 g (1 oz) sliced turkey
1 low-sodium turkey-bacon rasher, cooked
2 Cos lettuce leaves
4 slices tomato
1 apple

1. Spread pesto on 1 slice of bread. Top with turkey, bacon, lettuce, tomato and remaining bread slice. Cut sandwich in half using a sharp knife.

2. Serve sandwich with apple.

Serving size: 1 sandwich and 1 apple Calories 390; Fat 11g (sat 3g, mono 4g, poly 1g); Cholesterol 32mg; Protein 20g; Carbohydrate 60g; Sugars 23g; Fibre 10g; RS 2.6g; Sodium 614mg

Red Grape & Tuna Salad Pita

Tuna is a rich source of metabolism-boosting omega-3 fatty acids. Add that to the MUFAs in the almonds and the Resistant Starch in the pitta, and you've tripled the boost to your metabolism.

Prep: 7 minutes

Total time: 7 minutes

Makes: 1 serving

Resistant Starch:

1g

½ **75 g (3 oz) can tuna in water, drained**
100 g (3½ oz) red grapes, halved
1 tablespoon flaked almonds
1 tablespoon chopped fresh mint
1 tablespoon lemon juice
2 teaspoons olive oil
⅛ teaspoon black pepper
1 wholemeal pitta, halved

1. Combine first 7 ingredients in a small bowl. Toss gently. Serve in pitta halves.

Serving size: 2 stuffed pitta halves Calories 410; Fat 15g (sat 1.5g, mono 9g, poly 3g); Cholesterol 45mg; Protein 28g; Carbohydrate 45g; Sugars 14g; Fibre 6g; RS 1g; Sodium 700mg

Roast Beef Sandwich with Horseradish Aioli

The rye bread in this sandwich packs a good amount of Resistant Starch, and the veggies have plenty of fibre to keep you feeling satisfied all afternoon long.

Prep: 7 minutes

Total time: 7 minutes

Makes: 1 serving

Resistant Starch:

1.8g

2 tablespoons reduced-fat mayonnaise
2 teaspoons prepared horseradish
2 slices rye bread
2 (25 g/1 oz)) slices roast beef
25 g (1 oz) fresh spinach
150 g (5 oz) sliced cucumber
1 tablespoon less-sodium, low-fat Italian dressing

1. Combine mayonnaise and horseradish in a small bowl; stir well with a whisk.

2. Spread mayonnaise mixture on both bread slices. Top 1 bread slice with roast beef, spinach and remaining bread slice.

3. Serve with cucumber slices drizzled with dressing.

Serving size: 1 sandwich and 150 g (5 oz) cucumber salad Calories 359; Fat 10g (sat 2g, mono 3g, poly 4g); Cholesterol 38mg; Protein 24g; Carbohydrate 43g; Sugars 6g; Fibre 5g; RS 1.8g; Sodium 546mg

Smoked Salmon & Avocado Rolls

There's no raw seafood in this roll, so even those who avoid sushi for that reason can enjoy this. To save time, use the brown rice that you batch-cooked earlier in the week, or use a pre-cooked variety.

Prep: 10 minutes

Total time: 10 minutes

Makes: 1 serving

Resistant Starch: **2.6**g

¼ **avocado, mashed**
3 nori (seaweed) sheets
150 g (5 oz) cooked and cooled brown rice
1 (25 g/1 oz) slice smoked salmon
3 tomato slices
3 tablespoons chopped red onion
1 tablespoon capers

1. Spread avocado on nori sheets.

2. Top the avocado with brown rice, salmon, tomato, onion and capers; roll up the nori sheets. Slice rolls into pieces with a serrated knife.

Serving size: 3 rolls Calories 400; Fat 12g (sat 2g, mono 7g, poly 2.5g); Cholesterol 45mg; Protein 26g; Carbohydrate 47g; Sugars 3g; Fibre 9g; RS 2.6g; Sodium 430mg

Tuscan Barley Salad

Make sure to batch-cook barley earlier in the week to speed the prep time for this high-fibre, high–Resistant Starch dish. The orange zest adds a wonderful bright flavour to the salad, which tastes even better the next day.

Prep: 20 minutes
Cook: 5 minutes
Total time: 25 minutes
Makes: 4 servings

Resistant Starch:
3.8g

75 g (3 oz) chopped walnuts
1 navel orange
2 tablespoons olive oil
¼ teaspoon salt
600 g (1 lb 4 oz) cooked pearl barley
250 g (8 oz) fennel bulb, thinly sliced, plus 2 tablespoons chopped fennel fronds
4 tablespoons thinly sliced sun-dried tomatoes, packed in water

1. Toast walnuts in a nonstick frying pan over medium heat, stirring frequently to prevent scorching, 5 minutes or until fragrant. Transfer walnuts to a plate, and set aside.

2. Use a microplane grater or vegetable peeler to remove the zest from the orange (only the colourful skin, not the bitter white part underneath). If using a vegetable peeler, chop the zest finely; place zest in a large bowl. Carefully peel the orange with a knife, removing all the white pith and outer membrane. Hold the fruit over the bowl and cut between the inner membranes to release the orange segments; let them drop into the bowl, along with the juices. Use clean hands to tear larger segments into smaller pieces.

3. Add olive oil and salt; toss until combined. Add barley, fennel, sun-dried tomatoes and reserved walnuts. Toss until thoroughly combined.

Serving size: 250 g (8 oz) Calories 380; Fat 17g (sat 2g, mono 6.5g, poly 8g); Cholesterol 0mg; Protein 7g; Carbohydrate 54g; Sugars 5g; Fibre 9g; RS 3.8g; Sodium 230mg

★CarbStar★
BARLEY
1.9 grams of Resistant Starch per 75 g (3 oz)

In addition to Resistant Starch, barley is rich in soluble and insoluble fibre, which reduces appetite and keeps you regular. In one University of Minnesota study, participants reported significantly less hunger before lunch after they consumed a barley snack, compared with participants who consumed a snack made of refined rice.

Barley Risotto Primavera

Swapping the usual Arborio rice used in risotto for barley boosts fibre and Resistant Starch. Save prep time by batch-cooking the barley at the beginning of the week.

Prep: 15 minutes

Cook: 20 minutes

Total time: 35 minutes

Makes: 4 servings

Resistant Starch:
4.1g

2 tablespoons olive oil
2 carrots, peeled and chopped
½ small onion, finely chopped
2 garlic cloves, finely chopped
½ teaspoon dried thyme
450 g (15 oz) cooked quick-cooking barley
120 ml (4 fl oz) white wine (optional)
350–500 ml (12–16 fl oz) low-sodium vegetable stock, divided
1 small courgette, chopped
½ red pepper, chopped
½ yellow pepper, chopped
¼ teaspoon salt
Freshly ground black pepper, to taste
200 g (7 oz) frozen peas
75 g (3 oz) grated Parmesan cheese

1. Heat oil in a large nonstick frying pan over medium-high heat. Add carrot and onion, and cook 4–5 minutes until onion begins to brown. Add garlic and thyme; cook 1 minute or until fragrant.

2. Reduce heat to medium; stir in barley and white wine (if using) or 120 ml (4 fl oz); cook 1 minute or until liquid is absorbed. Add stock, peppers, and 180 ml (6 fl oz) stock; cook 4–5 minutes, stirring occasionally, until liquid is absorbed. Add remaining stock; cook until vegetables are tender and most of liquid has been absorbed. Add ¼ teaspoon salt and freshly ground black pepper.

3. Stir in peas; remove from heat. Let stand 1–2 minutes or until peas are thawed but still bright green. Stir in Parmesan just before serving.

Serving size: 400 g (14 oz) Calories 380; Fat 14g (sat 4g, mono 5g, poly 1g); Cholesterol 15mg; Protein 16g; Carbohydrate 50g; Sugars 5g; Fibre 9g; RS 4.1g; Sodium 620mg

Bistro-Style Steak with New Potatoes

Here's a classic, high-protein meal. Boiling the potatoes whole kicks the Resistant Starch factor up several notches.

Prep: 10 minutes

Cook: 25 minutes

Total time: 35 minutes

Makes: 4 servings

Resistant Starch: 2.3g

700 g (1 lb 8 oz) new potatoes
600 g (1 lb 4 oz) lean sirloin steak, trimmed of visible fat
½ teaspoon salt, divided
Freshly ground black pepper, to taste
6 teaspoons olive oil, divided
1 large shallot, finely chopped
120 ml (4 fl oz) dry red wine
150 g (5 oz) rocket, divided

1. Place potatoes in a large saucepan; cover with cold water. Bring water to the boil, and cook 15 minutes or until potatoes can be pierced with a fork. Drain and cool potatoes. Slice potatoes in half.

2. While potatoes cook, divide steak into 4 equal portions, and sprinkle with ¼ teaspoon salt and freshly ground black pepper. Heat 2 teaspoons oil in a large heavy frying pan over medium-high heat. Add steaks to pan, and cook 4–6 minutes per side or until a meat thermometer inserted into thickest part of the steak reads 71°C (160°F). Transfer steaks to a plate, and keep warm.

3. Reduce heat to medium-low; add 2 teaspoons oil and shallot to pan. Arrange potatoes, cut-sides down, in pan, and cook 5 minutes or until potatoes begin to brown.

4. Season with remaining ¼ teaspoon salt and freshly ground black pepper. Transfer potatoes to a bowl, and keep warm.

5. Increase heat to medium-high. Add wine, and gently scrape pan to loosen browned bits. Add remaining 2 teaspoons olive oil, and cook until liquid is reduced by half. Place a quarter of the rocket on each of 4 plates; divide steak and potatoes evenly. Top each serving with approximately 1 tablespoon sauce.

Serving size: 1 steak, 175 g (6 oz) potatoes, 40 g (1 ½ oz) rocket and 1 tablespoon sauce Calories 400; Fat 13g (sat 3g, mono 7g, poly 1g); Cholesterol 60mg; Protein 35g; Carbohydrate 30g; Sugars 3g; Fibre 4g; RS 2.3g; Sodium 390mg

Caribbean Mahi Mahi with Banana Chutney

Nearly every metabolism booster on *The CarbLover's Diet* is included in this recipe, with three Resistant Starch stars: brown rice, banana, and beans.

Prep: 15 minutes

Bake: 5 minutes

Total time: 20 minutes

Makes: 4 servings

Resistant Starch: **4.8g**

500 ml (16 fl oz) water
400 g (14 oz) uncooked quick-cooking brown rice
25 g (1 oz) flaked coconut
250 g (8 oz) canned kidney beans, rinsed and drained
¼ teaspoon salt
¼ teaspoon ground allspice
¼ teaspoon dried thyme
¼ teaspoon cayenne pepper
500 g (1 lb) skinless mahi mahi fillets, cut into 4 pieces
½ teaspoon olive oil
2 tablespoons mango chutney
2 bananas, peeled and chopped
1 spring onion, finely chopped
1 tablespoon chopped fresh coriander

1. Preheat grill.

2. Bring the water to the boil in a medium saucepan over medium-high heat.

3. If using boil-in-bag rice, drop in bag, and boil 10 minutes; remove from bag and add coconut. Reduce heat to low. Simmer, covered, 5 minutes. Turn off heat; stir in beans, and set aside. (If using regular quick-cooking brown rice, add rice and coconut to boiling water. Reduce heat to low. Simmer, covered, 5 minutes. Turn off heat; stir in beans, and set aside.)

4. While rice cooks, combine salt, allspice, thyme and cayenne pepper in a small bowl; set aside.

5. Arrange fish on a baking sheet. Drizzle oil over fish. Sprinkle half of seasoning mixture over fish; turn fish over and sprinkle with remaining seasoning.

6. Grill for 5–6 minutes or until fish flakes easily with a fork.

7. While fish cooks, combine chutney, banana, spring onions and coriander in a small bowl. Serve rice and bean mixture topped with fish and chutney mixture.

Serving size: 125 g (4 oz) mahi mahi, 175 g (6 oz) rice and beans, and about 4 tablespoons chutney Calories 410; Fat 4g (sat 2g, mono 1g, poly 0.5g); Cholesterol 85mg; Protein 29g; Carbohydrate 65g; Sugars 16g; Fibre 7g; RS 4.8g; Sodium 510mg

Fish Tacos with Sesame-Ginger Coleslaw

Corn tortillas add a hearty dose of Resistant Starch to this traditional Tex-Mex dish, while coleslaw lends fibre and crunch.

Prep: 10 minutes

Cook: 10 minutes

Total time: 20 minutes

Makes: 4 servings

Resistant Starch:
2.4g

700 g (1 lb 8oz) tilapia fillets
Cooking spray
¼ teaspoon salt
¼ teaspoon pepper
3 tablespoons natural low-fat Greek yogurt
2 tablespoons lime juice
1 tablespoon dark sesame oil
1 tablespoon low-sodium soy sauce
2 teaspoons grated peeled fresh ginger
1 teaspoon honey
350 g (12 oz) ready-made coleslaw mix
12 (15 cm/6 inch) corn tortillas, warmed

1. Heat a nonstick frying pan or griddle pan over medium heat. Coat fish with cooking spray; sprinkle with salt and pepper. Add fish to pan; cook 10–12 minutes, turning once, until fish flakes easily with a fork.

2. Combine yogurt and next 5 ingredients in a small bowl, stirring with a whisk. Combine dressing and coleslaw mix, tossing to coat.

3. Flake fish into pieces with a fork. Divide the fish between the tortillas. Top with coleslaw.

Serving size: 3 tacos Calories 390; Fat 9g (sat 2g, mono 3g, poly 3g); Cholesterol 85mg; Protein 40g; Carbohydrate 38g; Sugars 4g; Fibre 6g; RS 2.4g; Sodium 430mg

Mediterranean Seafood Grill with Skordalia

This dish includes a slice of sourdough bread in the garlicky potato sauce known as skordalia. This thick and creamy sauce can also be used as a spread on sandwiches or as a dip for veg and crackers.

Prep: 15 minutes
Cook: 40 minutes
Total time: 55 minutes
Makes: 4 servings

Resistant Starch: **1.7**g

500 g (1 lb) potatoes, peeled and diced
8 garlic cloves, peeled
1 slice sourdough bread, crust removed and torn into pieces
60 ml (2 fl oz) natural low-fat Greek yogurt
3 tablespoons olive oil, divided
Zest and juice of 1 lemon
½ teaspoon salt, divided
¼ teaspoon dried thyme
500 g (1 lb) halibut fillets, cut into 4 pieces
2 red peppers, quartered
500 g (1 lb) small courgettes, diagonally cut into 2.5 cm (1 inch) pieces
½ red onion, sliced

1. Place potatoes in a large saucepan, add garlic, cover with cold water, and cook over high heat 15 minutes or until potatoes are tender.

2. While the potatoes cook, place the bread in a large bowl. Spoon 2–3 tablespoons cooking liquid from potatoes over bread. Stir with a fork until smooth. Add yogurt, 2 tablespoons olive oil and lemon zest and juice; stir until a smooth paste forms.

3. Place a large bowl in the sink, and set a colander on top. Drain potatoes and garlic, reserving cooking liquid. Transfer potatoes to bread mixture, and mash until smooth. Add reserved cooking liquid 2 tablespoons at a time until mixture takes on the consistency of loose mashed potatoes. Stir in ¼ teaspoon salt and 2 teaspoons olive oil. Cover and keep warm.

4. Preheat griddle pan over medium-high heat. Drizzle fish with ½ teaspoon olive oil, and sprinkle with remaining ¼ teaspoon salt and thyme. Cook 2–3 minutes on each side or until fish flakes easily with a fork. Transfer to a plate; cover and keep warm.

5. Place pepper, courgette and red onion in a large bowl. Drizzle with remaining ½ teaspoon olive oil; toss to coat. Arrange the peppers in the griddle pan, and cook 5 minutes over medium heat. Add courgettes and onion; cook 10 minutes or until vegetables are tender, turning as necessary for even cooking.

6. Serve halibut with grilled vegetables and skordalia.

Serving size: 125 g (4 oz) halibut, ¼ of grilled vegetables, and 120 ml (4 fl oz) skordalia Calories 390; Fat 14g (sat 2g, mono 8g, poly 2g); Cholesterol 35mg; Protein 31g; Carbohydrate 37g; Sugars 7g; Fibre 5g; RS 1.7g; Sodium 280mg

Orecchiette with Cannellini Beans & Pesto

You can use any small pasta for this dish. Letting it cool to room temperature before serving will boost the Resistant Starch factor even higher.

Prep: 10 minutes

Cook: 15 minutes

Total time: 25 minutes

Makes: 4 servings

Resistant Starch:
4.4g

125 g (4 oz) uncooked orecchiette
1 teaspoon olive oil
2 garlic cloves, finely chopped
450 g (15 oz) can cannellini beans, rinsed
    and drained
3 plum tomatoes, chopped
100 ml (3 fl oz) prepared pesto
4 tablespoons grated Parmesan cheese

1. Cook pasta according to packet directions, omitting salt and fat.

2. While the pasta cooks, heat olive oil and garlic in a large nonstick frying pan over medium-high heat until garlic is fragrant. Add beans and tomato; reduce heat to low, and cook, stirring occasionally, about 5–7 minutes.

3. Drain pasta, and add to bean mixture. Add pesto; toss to combine. Divide evenly between 4 serving dishes. Top each serving with 1 table-spoon Parmesan.

Serving size: 175 g (6 oz) Calories 420; Fat 11g (sat 2.5g, mono 4g, poly 5g); Cholesterol 5mg; Protein 18g; Carbohydrate 63g; Sugars 5g; Fibre 7g; RS 4.4g; Sodium 360mg

Pan-Seared Scallops with Mexican Rice Salad

For an extra metabolism boost, feel free to add a kick of hot sauce, cayenne, jalapeños or chillies to this dish.

Prep: 20 minutes

Cook: 10 minutes

Total time: 30 minutes

Makes: 4 servings

Resistant Starch:

3.7g

1 lime
2 teaspoons olive oil, divided
1 teaspoon chilli powder, divided
¼ teaspoon salt, divided
450 g (15 oz) can low-sodium black beans, rinsed and drained
325 g (11 oz) can sweetcorn, drained
280 g (8 oz) cherry tomatoes, halved
50 g (2 oz) spring onions, chopped
2 tablespoons chopped fresh coriander
600 g (1 lb 4 oz) cooked brown rice
16 scallops

1. Squeeze juice from half the lime into a large bowl; add 1 teaspoon olive oil, ½ teaspoon chilli powder and ¼ teaspoon salt; stir well with a whisk. Add beans, sweetcorn, tomato, spring onions, and coriander; toss gently to combine. Stir in cooked rice and toss until thoroughly combined. Cover loosely and keep warm.

2. Combine remaining olive oil, chilli powder and salt in a large bowl. Pat scallops dry with kitchen paper and add to oil mixture, tossing until thoroughly coated. Squeeze 2 teaspoons juice from remaining lime half into a small bowl, and set aside.

3. Heat a large nonstick frying pan over medium-high heat. Arrange scallops in pan, flat sides down (make sure they aren't touching or they will steam, not sear properly). Cook 2–3 minutes on each side until lightly browned and opaque in the centre. Drizzle scallops with reserved lime juice, and toss gently to coat. Divide rice mixture evenly between 4 serving dishes and top each serving with 4 scallops. Serve immediately.

Serving size: 4 scallops and 350 g (12 oz) rice salad Calories 419; Fat 5g (sat 1g, mono 2g, poly 1g); Cholesterol 37mg; Protein 30g; Carbohydrate 64g; Sugars 4g; Fibre 9g; RS 3.7g; Sodium 497mg

Sirloin Salad with Blue Cheese Dressing & Sweet Potato Chips

Blue cheese? Steak? Chips?! Is this diet food? Yes, it is! By baking the chips, you slash calories without sacrificing flavour. Save time by using frozen sweet potato chips.

Prep: 10 minutes
Cook: 20 minutes
Total time: 30 minutes
Makes: 4 servings

Resistant Starch: **2.5g**

700 g (1 lb 8 oz) sweet potatoes, cut into 0.5 cm (¼ inch) thick matchsticks
500 g (1 lb) sirloin steak
Cooking spray
½ teaspoon salt, divided
½ teaspoon pepper, divided
120 ml (4 fl oz) natural low-fat Greek yogurt
4 tablespoons crumbled blue cheese
350 g (12 oz) chopped Cos lettuce
2 tomatoes, diced
2 carrots, peeled and grated

1. Preheat oven to 200°C/400°F/gas mark 6. Coat sweet potato chips and steak with cooking spray. Place on separate baking sheets and sprinkle with ¼ teaspoon each salt and pepper. Place chips and steak in oven for 20 minutes, turning chips once, halfway through. Steak is done when a meat thermometer inserted into the thickest part registers 71°C (160°F) (medium). Chips should be tender and crisp.

2. Combine yogurt, blue cheese and remaining salt and pepper. Toss lettuce, tomato and carrot together.

3. Cut steak into strips. Arrange the salad evenly on 4 plates and top with steak. Drizzle dressing over salad; serve with sweet potato chips.

Serving size: 150 g (5 oz) salad, 75 g (3 oz) steak, 175 g (6 oz) chips and 1 tablespoon dressing Calories 391; Fat 9g (sat 4g, mono 3g, poly 0.5g); Cholesterol 56mg; Protein 34g; Carbohydrate 44g; Sugars 12g; Fibre 8g; RS 2.5g; Sodium 393mg

Spanish-Style Prawns with Yellow Rice

Many Spanish dishes call for super-pricey saffron. To save money, we've substituted turmeric, a spice that lends a similar flavour and color for a fraction of the cost.

Prep: 10 minutes

Cook: 15 minutes

Total time: 25 minutes

Makes: 4 servings

Resistant Starch:

3.8g

4 garlic cloves, finely chopped
2 tablespoons olive oil, divided
1½ teaspoons smoked paprika
½ teaspoon salt, divided
500 g (1 lb) prawns, peeled and deveined
½ small onion, finely chopped
600 g (1 lb 4 oz) uncooked quick-cooking brown rice
½ teaspoon ground turmeric
600 ml (1 pint) cold water
75 g (3 oz) frozen peas
2 tablespoons dry sherry (optional)
1 tablespoon fresh chopped parsley

1. Combine garlic, 1 tablespoon olive oil, paprika and ¼ teaspoon salt in a large bowl; stir with a whisk. Add prawns, and toss to coat. Set aside.

2. Heat remaining oil in a large saucepan over medium-high heat. Add onion and cook 2–3 minutes until soft. Add rice, remaining salt and turmeric. Add the cold water; cover and reduce heat to low. Cook 4 minutes; remove from heat. Stir in peas, and let stand, covered, until ready to serve.

3. Heat a large nonstick frying pan over medium-high heat. Place prawns in centre of pan. Cook 2–3 minutes on each side or until opaque. Add sherry during the last minute of cooking, and toss to coat. Remove from heat. Fluff rice mixture and place on a serving platter. Arrange prawns on top of rice mixture, sprinkle with parsley and serve immediately.

Serving size: ¼ of shrimp and 200 g (7 oz) rice
Calories 430; Fat 10g (sat 1.5g, mono 5g, poly 2g); Cholesterol 170mg; Protein 31g; Carbohydrate 56g; Sugars 1g; Fibre 5g; RS 3.8g; Sodium 470mg

Seared Chicken Breasts with French Potato Salad

Double the amount of Resistant Starch in this dish by allowing the potato salad to cool to room temperature before serving.

Prep: 15 minutes

Cook: 20 minutes

Total time: 35 minutes

Makes: 4 servings

Resistant Starch: **2.3g**

700 g (1 lb 4 oz) small potatoes
125 g (4 oz) frozen whole green beans
2 tablespoons olive oil, divided
2 tablespoons chopped fresh parsley
1 tablespoon Dijon mustard
1 tablespoon cider vinegar
½ teaspoon salt, divided
Freshly ground black pepper
4 (150 g/5 oz) skinless, boneless chicken breasts
2 tablespoons plain flour
1 large shallot, finely chopped
4 tablespoons fresh lemon juice
½ teaspoon dried tarragon

1. Place potatoes in a large saucepan; cover with water. Bring water to the boil and cook 15 minutes or until potatoes can be easily pierced with a fork. Add green beans during last minute of cooking; drain and set aside.

2. While potatoes and beans cook, combine 1 tablespoon olive oil, parsley, mustard, vinegar and ¼ teaspoon salt in a large bowl; stir with a whisk. Season to taste with black pepper. When potatoes are cool enough to handle, slice larger pieces in half and add to bowl. Toss to coat and set aside.

3. Cover chicken breasts with greaseproof paper; pound to an even thickness using a mallet or small, heavy frying pan. Sprinkle with remaining salt and season with black pepper.

4. Place flour in a shallow dish; dredge chicken in flour. Heat remaining olive oil in a large nonstick frying pan over medium-high heat. Add chicken to pan, and cook 6–8 minutes or until chicken begins to brown; turn to brown other side. Add shallots, and cook 5–6 minutes or until a meat thermometer inserted into the thickest part of the chicken breast registers 74°C (165°F). Add lemon juice and tarragon, and turn chicken until evenly coated.

5. Place a chicken breast on each of 4 serving plates; serve with potato salad.

Serving size: 1 chicken breast and 200 g (7 oz) potato salad Calories 380; Fat 9g (sat 1.5g, mono 5g, poly 1g); Cholesterol 80mg; Protein 37g; Carbohydrate 37g; Sugars 3g; Fibre 5g; RS 2.3g; Sodium 490mg

Roasted Pork Fillet with Apricot-Barley Pilaf

Tossing the barley into the pan after the pork is cooked means that this dish doesn't waste a drop of flavour – and you'll have fewer dishes to wash afterwards, too.

Prep: 10 minutes
Cook: 30 minutes
Total time: 40 minutes
Makes: 4 servings

Resistant Starch:
2.9g

500 g (1 lb) pork fillet, trimmed of visible fat
1 teaspoon olive oil
¼ teaspoon salt
Freshly ground black pepper
2 tablespoons apricot jam
1 tablespoon less-sodium soy sauce
4 tablespoons pecans, coarsely chopped
1 celery stalk, finely chopped
1 carrot, peeled and diced
½ small onion, finely chopped
180 ml (6 fl oz) water
600 g (1 lb 4 oz) quick-cooking barley, cooked
75 g (3 oz) dried apricot halves, chopped
4 tablespoons chopped fresh parsley

1. Preheat oven to 190°C/375°F/gas mark 5.

2. Rub pork with olive oil; sprinkle with salt and pepper and set aside. Combine jam and soy sauce in a small bowl; set aside.

3. Heat a large ovenproof nonstick frying pan over medium-high heat. Add pecans, and cook, tossing frequently, 3–5 minutes or until fragrant.

4. Return pan to heat and add pork. Cook 5 minutes, turning every minute or two to brown evenly on all sides. Add jam mixture, celery, carrot and onion to pan; stir until jam melts and vegetables and pork are evenly coated with sauce. Stir in the water. Place pan in oven, and bake for 18–20 minutes or until a meat thermometer inserted into pork registers 71°C (160°F).

5. Remove pan from oven; transfer pork to plate. Cover loosely with foil, and let stand 5 minutes.

6. Stir barley, apricots and toasted pecans into vegetable mixture. (Remember the handle of the pan will be very hot!) Stir in parsley. Carefully slice pork into 12 equal pieces. Serve 3 slices pork on top of barley pilaf.

Serving size: 3 pieces pork and 175 g (6 oz) pilaf
Calories 400; Fat 9g (sat 1.5g, mono 4g, poly 2g); Cholesterol 75mg; Protein 28g; Carbohydrate 54g; Sugars 15g; Fibre 7g; RS 2.9g; Sodium 390mg

Roasted Vegetables & Italian Sausage with Polenta

We've shrunk the calorie count of this dish by using lean turkey sausage. To save time, use ready-prepared polenta

Prep: 20 minutes

COOK: 1 hour and 15 minutes

Total time: 1 hour and 35 minutes

Makes: 4 servings

Resistant Starch:
2 g

Cooking spray
1.2 litres (2¼ pints) water
175 g (6 oz) polenta
1 fennel bulb (about 250 g/8 oz), stem and fronds removed, sliced thin
1 yellow or orange pepper, sliced
½ red onion, sliced
500 g (1 lb) cherry tomatoes, halved
4 garlic cloves, crushed
1 tablespoon olive oil
½ teaspoon dried oregano
4 (125 g/4 oz) lean Italian turkey sausages
2 tablespoons fresh chopped parsley (optional)

1. Preheat oven to 220°C/425°F/gas mark 7.

2. Coat a 3 litre (5 pint) baking dish with cooking spray. Combine 1 litre (1¾ pints) water and polenta, and pour into prepared baking dish. Set aside.

3. Place fennel in a 23 x 33 cm (9 x 13 inch) baking dish. Add pepper, red onion, tomatoes and garlic. Drizzle with olive oil and sprinkle with oregano. Toss to coat. Arrange turkey sausages on top, and add the remaining water.

4. Bake sausage and vegetables, uncovered, for 20 minutes. Remove from oven; turn sausages, and toss vegetables. Place half of vegetable mixture on top of sausages before returning baking dish to oven.

5. Reduce temperature to 350°C/350°F/gas mark 4. Stir polenta mixture lightly, and place baking dish in oven. Bake for 45 minutes. Remove polenta from oven; stir gently with a fork, and return to oven. Bake both dishes an additional 10 minutes or until vegetables are completely soft and a thermometer inserted into the thickest part of a sausage registers 77°C (170°F). Remove from oven.

6. Stir polenta with a fork; polenta will continue to thicken as it stands. Serve polenta and sausage topped with vegetables and pan sauce. Sprinkle with parsley, if liked.

Serving size: 240 ml (8 fl oz) polenta, 1 sausage, 175 g (6 oz) vegetables and 2 tablespoons pan sauce Calories 390; Fat 14g (sat 3g, mono 2.5g, poly 0g); Cholesterol 76mg; Protein 25g; Carbohydrate 41g; Sugars 4g; Fibre 5g; RS 2g; Sodium 498mg

Thai Peanut Noodles

Supplying half your daily requirement for fibre, lots of appetite-suppressing protein, and some Resistant Starch and MUFAs, this quick-and-simple Asian-themed dish is just as slimming as it is satisfying.

Prep: 15 minutes
Cook: 15 minutes
Total time: 30 minutes
Makes: 4 servings

Resistant Starch: **2g**

250 g (8 oz) uncooked wholewheat linguine
500 g (1 lb) broccoli florets
150 g (5 oz) shelled frozen soya beans
120 ml (4 fl oz) peanut satay sauce
200 g (7 oz) bean sprouts
1 large carrot, peeled and grated
½ red pepper, cut into thin slices
4 tablespoons lightly salted, dry-roasted peanuts, chopped
Fresh lime wedges

1. Cook pasta according to packet directions, omitting salt and fat. During the last minute of cooking, add broccoli and soya beans. Drain well and transfer to a large bowl.

2. Add satay sauce to pasta mixture, and toss to coat. Add bean sprouts, carrot and pepper; toss until thoroughly combined. Divide pasta mixture evenly between 4 serving plates; top each serving with 1 tablespoon chopped peanuts. Serve with lime wedges.

Serving size: 300 g (10 oz) Calories 410; Fat 13g (sat 2g, mono 2g, poly 2g); Cholesterol 0mg; Protein 21g; Carbohydrate 61g; Sugars 8g; Fibre 14g; RS 2g; Sodium 610mg

Baked Two-Cheese Penne with Roasted Red Pepper Sauce

You'll love this twist on traditional macaroni cheese, and so will your kids. Cheese adds fat-burning CLA.

Prep: 10 minutes

Cook: 35 minutes

Total time: 45 minutes

Makes: 4 servings

Resistant Starch:

2g

Cooking spray
125 g (4 oz) uncooked wholewheat penne
2 tablespoons olive oil
2 tablespoons plain flour
½ teaspoon salt
¼ teaspoon freshly ground black pepper
350 ml (12 fl oz) 1% fat milk
25 g (1 oz) smoked Gouda, grated
50 g (2 oz) fontina cheese, grated
4 tablespoons panko (Japanese breadcrumbs)
8 tablespoons roasted red pepper
1 tablespoon natural low-fat Greek yogurt

1. Heat oven to 180°C/350°F/gas mark 4. Coat a 20 cm (8 inch) square baking dish with cooking spray; set aside.

2. Bring a large pan of water to the boil over high heat; add pasta, and cook 7 minutes or until al dente. Drain and set aside.

3. Reduce heat to medium, and add olive oil to pan. Add flour, salt and pepper; cook 1–2 minutes until flour begins to brown. Stir in milk, 120 ml (4 fl oz) at a time, whisking well to ensure a smooth sauce. Stir in cheeses; whisk until completely melted. Stir in cooked pasta. Transfer mixture to prepared baking dish.

4. Top pasta mixture with panko; bake in preheated oven for 20 minutes or until top begins to brown and cheese is bubbly.

5. While pasta mixture bakes, place roasted peppers and yogurt in a blender or food processor; process until smooth. Cut baked pasta evenly into 4 pieces, and place on 4 serving dishes; drizzle each serving with roasted red pepper sauce.

Serving size: ¼ of penne and 2 tablespoons sauce
Calories 433; Fat 16g (sat 6g, mono 7g, poly 1g); Cholesterol 29mg; Protein 17g; Carbohydrate 56g; Sugars 8g; Fibre 5g; RS 2g; Sodium 528mg

Bacon, Pear & Gorgonzola Pizza

If you don't want to
make your own pizza
dough, go ahead
and use prepared
– or even a
wholemeal pitta
bread.

Prep: 15 minutes

Cook: 20 minutes

Total time: 35 minutes

Makes: 4 servings

Resistant
Starch:

1.6g

250 g (8 oz) shop-bought pizza dough (or make your
   own with our recipe on the next page)
75 g (3 oz) low-fat ricotta cheese
1 tablespoon honey
50 g (2 oz) low-fat grated mozzarella cheese, divided
1 pear, halved, cored, and thinly sliced
50 g (2 oz) ham, finely chopped
4 tablespoons chopped walnuts
2 tablespoons crumbled gorgonzola or other blue cheese
250 g (8 oz) mixed salad leaves, divided
500 g (1 lb) broccoli florets, divided
6 tablespoons low-fat balsamic vinaigrette, divided

1. Preheat oven to 200°/400°/gas mark 6.

2. With a floured rolling pin, roll dough into a 30 cm (12 inch) circle; transfer to a 30 cm (12 inch) pizza stone or round baking dish. Bake in preheated oven for 5–7 minutes or until crust begins to puff.

3. While base bakes, stir together ricotta cheese and honey. Remove base from oven, and flip so bottom is now on top. Spread ricotta mixture evenly over base. Top with half the mozzarella, the pear, ham and walnuts. Top with remaining mozzarella and gorgonzola.

4. Return pizza to oven; bake an additional 15 minutes until cheese is melted and bubbly. Allow pizza to set before slicing into 8 pieces.

5. While pizza bakes, assemble side salads, using a quarter of the salad leaves, broccoli and dressing for each serving.

Serving size: 2 slices pizza and 175 g (6 oz) salad Calories 360; Fat 13g (sat 4.5g, mono 3g, poly 4g); Cholesterol 24mg; Protein 17g; Carbohydrate 46g; Sugars 12g; Fibre 7g; RS 1.6g; Sodium 504mg

Pizza Dough

Prep: 10 minutes with 1 hour rising time

Total time: 1 hour 10 minutes

Makes: 700 g (1 lb 8 oz) dough (enough for 3 thin 30 cm/12 inch pizzas; 12 servings)

240 ml (8 fl oz) warm water (about 43°C/110 °F)
2 teaspoons (about 1 sachet) fast action dry yeast
1 teaspoon sugar
250 g (8 oz) plain flour
175 g (6 oz) wholemeal flour
½ teaspoon salt
1 tablespoon olive oil, divided

1. Combine warm water, yeast and sugar in a small bowl; let stand about 10 minutes or until yeast begins to foam.

2. Combine flours and salt in bowl of a mixer fitted with a dough hook. Add yeast mixture and 2 teaspoons olive oil. Mix on low speed 2–3 minutes or until dough has formed a ball and no longer feels sticky. Coat dough and insides of bowl with remaining 1 teaspoon olive oil. Cover with a towel, and let rise in a warm place (30°C/85°F), free from draughts, about 1 hour or until doubled in size.

3. Refrigerate unused dough for up to 3 days in a zip-top plastic bag.

Coconut-Date Truffles

For best results, use Medjool dates for this recipe; they are extra plump and moist. You can store leftover truffles covered in the fridge for up to 10 days.

Prep: 10 minutes

Total time: 10 minutes

Makes: 4 servings

Resistant Starch:
0.2g

8 dates, pitted and chopped
8 tablespoons puffed-wheat cereal
2 tablespoons dessicated coconut

1. Place dates in a large bowl. Mash with fingers until dates form a ball.

2. Add cereal; knead into dates.

3. Form into 8 balls; roll each in coconut to coat.

Serving size: 2 truffles Calories 160; Fat 2g (sat 1.5g, mono 0g, poly 0g); Cholesterol 0mg; Protein 1g; Carbohydrate 38g; Sugars 32g; Fibre 4g; RS 0.2g; Sodium 0mg

Pea & Walnut Hummus

Usually, hummus is made from chickpeas, but this version uses green peas, which are packed with Resistant Starch and fibre.

Prep: 10 minutes

Total time: 10 minutes

Makes: 4 servings

150 g (5 oz) frozen peas, thawed
4 tablespoons chopped walnuts
2 tablespoons fresh lemon juice
1 garlic clove, finely chopped
½ teaspoon salt
½ teaspoon pepper
8 rye crackers

1. Combine first 6 ingredients (through pepper) in a blender or food processor; process until smooth.

2. Serve with crackers.

Serving size: 2 tablespoons hummus and 2 crackers
Calories 150; Fat 5g (sat 0g, mono 0.5g, poly 3.5g); Cholesterol 0mg; Protein 5g; Carbohydrate 23g; Sugars 1g; Fibre 5g; RS 1.4g; Sodium 340mg

Cannellini Bean Salsa & Chips

This easy snack gets you almost a third of your way to your Resistant Starch goal for the day. It serves four, so make up a batch, and store leftovers, covered, in the fridge.

Prep: 10 minutes

Total time: 10 minutes

Makes: 4 servings

Resistant Starch: 3g

450 g (15 oz) can cannellini beans, rinsed and drained
2 tablespoons fresh lime juice
¼ teaspoon salt
1 plum tomato, diced
2 spring onions, finely diced
20 corn chips

1. Combine beans, juice and salt in a bowl. Mash with a potato masher until semi-smooth.

2. Add tomato and spring onions; stir to blend. Serve with corn chips.

Serving size: 60 ml (2 fl oz) salsa and 5 chips
Calories 170; Fat 4g (sat 0.5g, mono 0, poly 0g); Cholesterol 0mg; Protein 7g; Carbohydrate 20g; Sugars 1g; Fibre 5g; RS 3g; Sodium 230mg

The *CarbLover's* Recipe Collection **199**

Garlic & Herb Yogurt Dip

If you wish, use natural low-fat yogurt instead of the thicker, creamier Greek yogurt. Store leftover dip, covered, in the fridge for up to three days.

Prep: 5 minutes

Total time: 5 minutes

Makes: 4 serving

Resistant Starch: 1g

180 ml (6 fl oz) natural low-fat Greek yogurt
1 garlic clove, finely chopped
2 tablespoons chopped chives
¼ teaspoon salt
¼ teaspoon pepper
¼ teaspoon dried dill
1 tablespoon lemon juice
125 g (4 oz) baked potato crisps

1. Combine first 7 ingredients in a small bowl. Serve with crisps.

Serving size: 3 tablespoons dip and 25 g (1 oz) crisps (about 12 crisps) Calories 160; Fat 6g (sat 1.5g, mono 3g, poly 1g); Cholesterol 5mg; Protein 5g; Carbohydrate 23g; Sugars 3g; Fibre 1g; RS 1g; Sodium 420mg

Chilli-Spiked Pitta Chips

These spicy chips will jump-start your metabolism, satisfy your craving for something crunchy, and supply you with a little Resistant Starch, too.

Prep: 5 minutes

Cook: 5 minutes

Total time: 10 minutes

Makes: 1 serving

Resistant Starch:

1g

**1 wholemeal pitta
Cooking spray
¼ teaspoon chilli powder**

1. Coat pitta with cooking spray; sprinkle with chilli powder. Cut pitta into 6 triangles.

2. Toast triangles on baking sheet under the grill for 5 minutes, turning once, until golden and crunchy.

Serving size: 6 pitta chips Calories 160; Fat 3.5g (sat 0g, mono 0g, poly 1g); Cholesterol 0mg; Protein 6g; Carbohydrate 28g; Sugars 2g; Fibre 4g; RS 1g; Sodium 330mg

Sunflower-Lentil Spread

Lentils are a powerhouse provider of Resistant Starch. In this recipe, they help you get nearly a third of your way to your daily 10-gram goal.

Prep: 10 minutes
Total time: 10 minutes
Makes: 4 servings

Resistant Starch: **3.1**g

450 g (15 oz) can lentils, rinsed and drained
1 tablespoon lemon juice
¼ teaspoon salt
¼ teaspoon pepper
2 tablespoons sunflower seeds
1 celery stalk, finely diced
1 spring onion, finely diced
2 tablespoons chopped fresh parsley
2 pittas, halved

1. Combine lentils, juice, salt and pepper in a blender; process until smooth. Stir in sunflower seeds, celery, spring onion and parsley.

2. Microwave pitta halves on HIGH 1 minute. Serve with spread.

Serving size: 4 tablespoons spread and ½ pitta
Calories 180; Fat 3g (sat 0g, mono 1g, poly 1.5g); Cholesterol 0mg; Protein 10g; Carbohydrate 29g; Sugars 3g; Fibre 10g; RS 3.1g; Sodium 430mg

Creamy Sweet Potato Dip

The chipotle chilli powder in this sweet and spicy snack will rev your metabolism, while the sweet potato fills you up with Resistant Starch. Speed prep time by using the sweet potato you batch-cooked earlier in the week.

Prep: 5 minutes

Bake: 10 minutes

Total time: 15 minutes

Makes: 1 serving

Resistant Starch: **2.1g**

½ **wholemeal pitta, split and cut into 8 pieces**
5 **tablespoons roasted mashed sweet potato**
1 **tablespoon natural low-fat Greek yogurt**
¼ **teaspoon honey**
⅛ **teaspoon dried chipotle chilli powder**
⅛ **teaspoon salt**

1. Preheat oven to 180°C/350°F/gas mark 4. Arrange pitta pieces on a baking sheet; bake in oven for 10 minutes until crisp.

2. While pitta bakes, combine sweet potato, yogurt, honey, chilli powder and salt in a small bowl; stir with a fork until smooth. Serve with warm pitta chips.

Serving size: 5 tablespoons dip and 8 chips Calories 170; Fat 1g (sat 0g, mono 0g, poly 0.5g); Cholesterol 0mg; Protein 6g; Carbohydrate 35g; Sugars 9g; Fibre 5g; RS 2.1g; Sodium 490mg

Warm Pear with Cinnamon Ricotta

This snack is rich in both fibre and CLA. The cinnamon is rich in antioxidants and may help control blood sugar, too.

Prep: 5 minutes

Cook: 10 minutes

Total time: 15 minutes

Makes: 1 serving

1 small pear, halved and cored
4 tablespoons low-fat ricotta cheese
¼ teaspoon cinnamon

1. Preheat grill. Place pear on a baking sheet; grill 10–12 minutes until tender.

2. Combine ricotta and cinnamon in a small bowl. Top warm pear with ricotta mixture.

Serving size: 1 pear and 4 tablespoons topping
Calories 170; Fat 5g (sat 3g, mono 1.5g, poly 0g); Cholesterol 20mg; Protein 8g; Carbohydrate 27g; Sugars 15g; Fibre 5g; RS 0g; Sodium 80mg

Cheddar & Apple Melt

In this recipe, sliced apple adds crunch and fibre to a traditional cheese quesadilla.

Prep: 5 minutes
Cook: 5 minutes
Total time: 10 minutes
Makes: 1 serving

Resistant Starch: **0.8g**

1 small apple, thinly sliced
1 (15 cm/6 inch) corn tortilla
1 tablespoon grated Cheddar cheese

1. Place apple slices on tortilla. Sprinkle with cheese.

2. Microwave at HIGH 30 seconds until cheese is bubbly. Cut into quarters.

Serving size: 1 melt Calories 160; Fat 3.5g (sat 1.5g, mono 1g, poly 0.5g); Cholesterol 5mg; Protein 4g; Carbohydrate 31g; Sugars 16g; Fibre 5g; RS 0.8g; Sodium 55mg

SUPER SIMPLE *CARBLOVER'S* SNACKS

Easy-to-make snacks are key to **CarbLover's** plan. The 8 snacks listed below can be assembled in about 3 minutes and pack about 150 calories each. They keep your energy up between meals and prevent you from overeating all day.

1. Antipasto Platter: On a serving plate, arrange 12 canned black olives, drained; 8 tablespoons bottled marinated artichoke hearts, drained; and ½ of a bottled roasted red pepper, sliced.

2. Pistachio & Dried Cherry Crostini: Combine 2 tablespoons low-fat cottage cheese with 1 teaspoon honey, 2 teaspoons chopped pistachios, and 2 teaspoons chopped dried cherries; serve on top of 2 rye crispbreads.

3. Brie & Apple Slices: Enjoy 1 small sliced apple with 25 g (1 oz) Brie.

4. Fig & Flax Yogurt: Mix 120 ml (4 fl oz) natural low-fat Greek yogurt with 1 teaspoon honey, 3 chopped dried figs and 1 teaspoon ground flaxseed.

5. Greek Yogurt with Marmalade & Walnuts: Combine 120 ml (4 fl oz) natural low-fat Greek yogurt with 2 teaspoons 100 per cent fruit orange marmalade and 1 tablespoon chopped walnuts.

6. Honey-Curried Yogurt Dip with Carrots & Broccoli: Combine 120 ml (4 fl oz) natural low-fat Greek yogurt with 1 teaspoon honey, ¼ teaspoon curry powder and ⅛ teaspoon salt; serve with 125 g (4 oz) each baby carrots and broccoli florets.

7. Hummus with Feta & Dill: Top 4 tablespoons shop-bought hummus with 1 tablespoon feta cheese and ⅛ teaspoon dried dill; serve with 150 g (5 oz) sliced cucumber.

8. Salmon & Cream Cheese Bites: Spread 2 teaspoons low-fat cream cheese on 1 slice toasted pumpernickel bread; top with 15 g (½ oz) smoked salmon and 2 teaspoons chopped chives.

Banana Ice Cream

Home-made ice cream is easier than you ever imagined! More important, this version is low in sugar and calories and high in omega-3s, fibre, and Resistant Starch.

Prep: 5 minutes

Total time: 5 minutes

Makes: 1 serving

Resistant Starch:

4g

1 small banana, peeled, sliced and frozen
3 tablespoons 1% fat milk
1 tablespoon chopped walnuts

1. Place frozen banana pieces and milk in a blender or food processor; process until thick. Top with walnuts.

Serving size: 120 ml (4 fl oz) Calories 160; Fat 6g (sat 1g, mono 1g, poly 3.5g); Cholesterol 0mg; Protein 4g; Carbohydrate 26g; Sugars 15g; Fibre 3g; RS 4g; Sodium 20mg

Chocolate-Dipped Banana Bites

Chocolate is a rich source of metabolism-boosting MUFAs, and bananas are the richest source of Resistant Starch there is, making this dessert a weight-loss winner.

Prep: 5 minutes
Cook: 5 minutes
Total time: 10 minutes
Makes: 1 serving

Resistant Starch:

4g

2 tablespoons plain chocolate chips
1 small banana, peeled and cut into 2.5 cm (1 inch) chunks

1. Place chocolate chips in a small microwave-safe bowl. Microwave on HIGH 1 minute or until chocolate melts. Dip half of each banana piece in melted chocolate. Serve immediately.

Serving size: 1 banana Calories 190; Fat 7g (sat 4g, mono 2g, poly 0.5g); Cholesterol 0mg; Protein 2g; Carbohydrate 36g; Sugars 24g; Fibre 4g; RS 4g; Sodium 0mg

Dark Chocolate & Oat Clusters

What's not to love about chocolate and peanut butter, especially when both are high in MUFAs? As a bonus, the oats provide Resistant Starch.

Prep: 5 minutes
Cook: 3 minutes
Stand: 10 minutes
Total time: 18 minutes
Makes: 4 servings

Resistant Starch:
1.7 g

2 tablespoons peanut butter
2 tablespoons 1% fat milk
4 tablespoons plain chocolate chips
75 g (3 oz) rolled oats

1. Heat peanut butter, milk and chocolate chips in a saucepan over low heat 3 minutes or until chips melt.

2. Stir in oats. Remove from heat.

3. With a spoon, small ice-cream scoop or melon baller, drop 8 ball-shaped portions on a greaseproof paper–lined baking sheet. Let set in fridge for 10 minutes before serving.

Serving size: 2 clusters Calories 160; Fat 8g (sat 3g, mono 3.5g, poly 1.5g); Cholesterol 0mg; Protein 5g; Carbohydrate 19g; Sugars 7g; Fibre 3g; RS 1.7g; Sodium 40mg

Chocolate-Orange Spoonbread

Resistant Starch-rich polenta gives this dish a deliciously creamy texture.

Prep: 5 minutes

Cook: 45 minutes

Total time: 50 minutes

Makes: 6 servings

Resistant Starch: 1g

1 tablespoon unsalted butter
75 g (3 oz) sugar
150 g (5 oz) fine polenta
600 ml (1 pint) cold water
75 g (3 oz) 70 % cocoa solids dark chocolate, chopped
Zest of 1 orange
Orange slices for garnish, optional

1. Preheat oven to 180°C/350°F/gas mark 4.

2. Spread butter along bottom and sides of a 3 litre (5 pint) baking dish. Add sugar, polenta and cold water; stir well with a whisk. Bake in preheated oven for 30 minutes. Remove from oven, and stir mixture carefully with a fork or whisk until smooth; bake an additional 15 minutes.

3. Remove from oven, and stir until smooth. Add chocolate; stir until chocolate melts completely. Garnish with zest, and serve warm or at room temperature with a slice of orange, if liked.

Serving size: 80 ml (3 fl oz) Calories 200; Fat 8g (sat 5g, mono 2g, poly 0g); Cholesterol 5mg; Protein 2g; Carbohydrate 29g; Sugars 14g; Fibre 4g; RS 1 g; Sodium 12mg

Quick Mango-Coconut Sorbet

It takes almost no time to make this easy mango sorbet – and it's rich in both fibre and CLA.

Prep: 5 minutes

Total time: 5 minutes

Makes: 1 serving

125 g (4 oz) frozen mango chunks
3 tablespoons 1% fat milk
1 teaspoon honey
2 teaspoons dessicated coconut, toasted

1. Place mango, milk and honey in a blender or food processor; process until thick. Top with coconut.

Serving size: 120 ml (4 fl oz) Calories 160; Fat 3g (sat 2.5g, mono 0g, poly 0g); Cholesterol 0mg; Protein 3g; Carbohydrate 33g; Sugars 29g; Fibre 3g; RS 0g; Sodium 20mg

Maple Brown Rice Pudding

This recipe uses Resistant Starch-rich brown rice instead of the usual white. To save time, use a fast-cooking brown rice. The almonds pack metabolism-boosting MUFAs, too, and the cinnamon may help steady blood sugar.

Prep: 5 minutes

Cook: 6 minutes

Total time: 11 minutes

Makes: 4 servings

Resistant Starch: **1.3g**

300 g (10 oz) cooked brown rice
120 ml (4 fl oz) 1% fat milk
3 tablespoons maple syrup
½ teaspoon ground cinnamon
4 tablespoons sliced almonds

1. Combine the rice, milk, maple syrup and cinnamon in a microwave-safe bowl.

2. Microwave at HIGH 6–8 minutes, stirring occasionally, until most of the milk is absorbed. Stir and top with almonds.

Serving size: 120 ml (4 fl oz) Calories 170; Fat 4g (sat 0.5g, mono 2g, poly 1g); Cholesterol 0mg; Protein 4g; Carbohydrate 30g; Sugars 11g; Fibre 2g; RS 1.3g; Sodium 15mg

Merlot Strawberries with Whipped Cream

Who says wine is just for drinking? You can make an amazing dessert sauce with wine in minutes. Don't worry about getting tipsy: Boiling the sauce removes about 85 per cent of the alcohol.

Prep: 5 minutes

Cook: 5 minutes

Total time: 10 minutes

Makes: 4 servings

120 ml (4 fl oz) merlot
2 tablespoons fresh lemon juice
2 tablespoons honey
¼ teaspoon vanilla extract
500 g (1 lb) strawberries, sliced
240 ml (8 fl oz) cream, whipped

1. Bring merlot, juice and honey to the boil in a saucepan over high heat. Remove from heat; stir in vanilla.

2. Drizzle sauce over sliced berries. Top with whipped cream.

Serving size: 125 g (4 oz) berries, 4 tablespoons whipped cream and 2 tablespoons wine sauce
Calories 140; Fat 3.5g (sat 2g, mono 1g, poly 0.5g); Cholesterol 10mg; Protein 1g; Carbohydrate 22g; Sugars 16g; Fibre 3g; RS 0g; Sodium 20mg

Sweet Potato Pudding

Since sweet potatoes are packed with natural sugar, this recipe requires just a bit of honey. Speed prep time by using the sweet potato you batch-cooked earlier in the week.

Prep: 15 minutes
Cook: 25 minutes
Total time: 40 minutes
Makes: 6 servings

Resistant Starch:
1.7g

Cooking spray
2 large eggs
4 tablespoons honey, divided
4 tablespoons 1% fat milk
1 slice wholemeal bread, crusts removed
500 ml (16 fl oz) mashed baked sweet potato
1 teaspoon vanilla extract
½ teaspoon ground cinnamon
¼ teaspoon ground allspice
2 tablespoons chopped pecans
2 tablespoons chopped crystallized ginger
4 tablespoons low-fat Greek yogurt

1. Preheat oven to 180°C/350°F/gas mark 4. Coat a 1.5 litre (2¾ pint) baking dish with cooking spray.

2. Combine eggs, 3 tablespoons honey, milk and bread in a large bowl. Beat with a hand blender at medium speed until smooth. Add sweet potato, vanilla, cinnamon and allspice; beat until smooth. Pour mixture into prepared baking dish. Sprinkle pecans and ginger over top. Bake in preheated oven for 25 minutes or until pudding is set and slightly puffy. (It will sink slightly as it cools.)

3. While pudding bakes, combine yogurt and remaining 1 tablespoon honey; stir until smooth. Divide pudding between 4 serving bowls; top each serving evenly with yogurt mixture.

Serving size: 75 g (3 oz) pudding and 2 teaspoons topping Calories 200; Fat 4g (sat 1g, mono 2g, poly 1g); Cholesterol 70mg; Protein 6g; Carbohydrate 38g; Sugars 20g; Fibre 3g; RS 1.7g; Sodium 95mg

Raspberries with Chocolate Yogurt Mousse

Cocoa powder adds MUFAs, the yogurt is rich in CLA, and the raspberries pack plenty of fibre to make this a guilt-free treat.

Prep: 5 minutes

Total time: 5 minutes

Makes: 1 serving

120 ml (4 fl oz) natural low-fat Greek yogurt
1 tablespoon cocoa powder
1 tablespoon honey
25 g (1 oz) fresh raspberries

1. Combine yogurt, cocoa and honey in a serving bowl. Stir until blended. Top with raspberries.

Serving size: 120 ml (4 fl oz) yogurt and 25 g (1 oz) berries Calories 170; Fat 3g (sat 2g, mono 0g, poly 0g); Cholesterol 10mg; Protein 11g; Carbohydrate 29g; Sugars 23g; Fibre 4g; RS 0g; Sodium 40mg

CARBLOVER'S SMART RECIPE SWAPS

You know how some books teach you "makeover" techniques that turn an unhealthy recipe into a healthy one? The same principle applies here, but instead we show you how to "carb it up". It's fun to get creative and put a CarbLover's stamp on all of your personal recipes.

SWAP THIS out	SWAP THIS in
Shop-bought croutons	Toasted rye, pumpernickel or sourdough bread; roasted potato cubes; baked polenta cubes
White rice	Brown rice
Plain white flour	Wholemeal flour: Replace up to one-third of plain flour with regular wholemeal flour.
White pasta	Wholewheat or fibre-fortified pasta
Mayonnaise (for spreads and dips)	Hummus, mashed avocado, low-fat Greek or regular yogurt, mashed cannellini beans, puréed low-fat cottage cheese, puréed sweet potato, puréed green peas, or skordalia (page 175)
Breadcrumbs (for coating meat and fish)	Crumbled potato crisps, cornflakes, puffed-wheat cereal or crushed nuts
Butter	Mashed banana or dates. Start out by swapping half the butter for the same amount of mashed fruit. You might have to decrease other liquid ingredients in the recipe to get it just right.
Minced beef	Substitute beans for up to half of the minced beef in a recipe.

"I Lost Weight on *CarbLover's*"

BEFORE

LUCY PASTRANA

Age: **45**
Height: **1.68 m (5' 6")**
Weight before: **106.1 kg (16 st 10 lb)**
Weight after: **94.3 kg (14 st 12 lb)**
Weight lost: **11.8 kg (26 lb)**

Biggest success moment: The day my son came home with 18 Dunkin' Donuts! The old me would have eaten one; the new me chose a banana and almond butter.

Biggest challenge: Overeating before my period. I crave sweets for an entire week!

Favourite recipe: Fish Tacos with Sesame-Ginger Slaw (page 172). The creamy slaw makes it taste like a takeaway meal!

AFTER

I started CarbLover's because I wanted to weigh less than 90 kg (200 lb) again. My weight has yo-yoed my entire life, from 68 kg (10 st 10 lb) 23 years ago, just before I got married, to 113 kg (17 st 12 lb) , after a tough year recently. I've tried Slim-Fast, Atkins, even the "cabbage soup" diet, but nothing helped. Within a month of beginning CarbLover's, I was introduced to wholegrain foods I'd never tried, like brown rice and polenta. These ingredients eased my cravings. I realized the lack of fibre in my usual snack fare – crisps, doughnuts or biscuits – was making me eat way more sugar and sodium.

The most surprising part of this diet was the increase in my energy. I started taking an hour-long Zumba class after work. Before, I'd be exhausted after the class, eat a big snack, and fall asleep by 9:30. Now, dinner keeps me full, and I have no problem staying up until 11 cleaning my kitchen and reading. I feel as though I'm drinking a cup of coffee!

CarbLover's taught me that as long as I have the right combination of vegetables, protein and Resistant Starch, I won't feel hungry. And it can be on my terms. I created an alternative to the Courgette & Potato Scramble with Bacon (page 137) by mixing sweet potato, bits of pork loin, egg whites and spinach. Bottom line: At this point, I don't look at this diet as having a beginning, middle and end. I see it as indulging in the healthy stuff for life. With only 8 pounds left to go, I'm confident I'll be less than 200 pounds by my 46th birthday!

Chapter 8

Reach your *CarbLover's* Goal Faster

YOU'RE FOUR WEEKS into *The CarbLover's Diet,* and it's time to reflect on your many successes. Chances are your waistband is a lot looser. You're glowing (have you been getting compliments on your clear skin, bright eyes and shiny hair? It's probably those carbs). Your mood is good – you feel less stressed, more energized than you have in years. Rather than obsessing over how little or how much you're eating, you're in a regular meal groove, enjoying the flavour, texture and just plain yumminess of your favourite foods. Best of all, **you've lost up to 5.5 kg (12 lb)**. If that's your final goal weight, congratulations! You can skip these pages and go directly to Chapter 10 for advice on maintaining your weight loss forever.

But if you want to lose 5, 10, even 40 or more kg (15, 35, 100 lb) – here are two things I want you to do:

● Continue the 21-Day CarbLover's Immersion Plan, but cut out one snack;

● Follow the Get-to-Goal Strategies below. These simple tricks will help you lose weight even faster by zapping a few hundred extra calories a day. Try to incorporate at least two or even more of these into your life to really get the scales moving. Finally, only choose those strategies that you can actually stick with. Hate green tea or just can't make time for 8 hours' sleep a night? Do something else that you can commit to!

9 GET-TO-GOAL STRATEGIES THAT REALLY WORK

1. Automate eating.

Some people can lose weight while enjoying lots of variety in their food choices, while others discover that variety only stimulates their appetite. Frances Largeman-Roth, RD, calls this the "buffet effect" (you know, where you just ... can't ... stop eating because there are so many options?). There's some evidence that backs up this theory: When researchers at The University of Illinois at Urbana-Champaign offered study participants M&Ms in 10 different colours, they gobbled up 77 per cent more sweets than when offered just seven colours. In another study done by the same researchers, participants consumed 55 per cent more jelly beans when they were offered 24 varieties of flavours versus only 6 varieties.[1] If you suspect too many different "tastes" makes you hungrier, try this: Instead of eating seven different breakfasts, lunches, dinners and snacks each week, you may want to try alternating between just two or three of them. Dieters who have tried it say they actually appreciate having to make fewer decisions and feel fuller faster.

2. Control portions with frozen meals.

Replacing two or more dinners a week with frozen meals can be helpful when it comes to portion control: Since these kinds of meals are already portioned for you, there's no guesswork – and no chance you'll be tempted to have seconds or thirds.

3. Cool your food.

If you enjoyed cold pizza or spaghetti for breakfast as a student, now's a good time to get back to the habit. Cold foods are thought to help you to burn more fat and fill up on fewer calories. Cooking actually reduces the amount of Resistant Starch in a food because it causes the starch to absorb water and swell, breaking up the starch and making it more digestible. As a food cools, however, the starch recrystallizes back into Resistant Starch. This is why a cold boiled potato has twice as much Resistant Starch as a hot one. Eating cold, high-Resistant Starch foods may fill you up faster, so you don't need to eat everything on your plate. It will also provide you with an extra metabolism boost.[2]

4. Choose less-ripe fruit.

As fruit ripens, starch turns into sugar. This is why a green banana has 12.5 grams of Resistant Starch, whereas a ripe one has just 4.7 grams. Bottom line: The less ripe your fruit, the more Resistant Starch it will contain – and the more fat you'll burn.

5. Cook al dente.

The more a food is cooked, the more water the starch absorbs, causing the starch to become more digestible (which may hinder weight loss). This is why al dente foods are thought to offer you more slimming Resistant Starch than foods that have been cooked into limpness.[3]

6. Substitute pepper for salt.

You know how you feel hot after a spicy meal? You're burning fat thanks to **capsaicin**, a substance in chilli peppers that speeds metabolism. Some recipes in Chapter 7 contain cayenne and other hot spices, but if you want to boost your weight loss even more, try sprinkling a little hot pepper on whatever you want.

7. Sip more green tea.

I hope you're already sipping my tried-and-true tea-based Fat-Flushing Cocktail on page 64. If not, consider this: Green tea packs two key metabolism boosters, and more tea could equal bigger weight loss. In one study, participants who consumed caffeinated green tea daily continued to lose weight after four weeks, whereas study participants who did not have the drink had significant weight regain. Other research has found that drinking a cup of green tea before your workout can increase your fat-burning during it. Very high amounts of green tea (the amount in several cups) has been shown to boost fat-burning up to 17 per cent.[4, 5]

8. Sleep an extra hour every night.

You really can sleep your way to a smaller waistline, and an hour or two more zzzs can make all the difference. When you don't get enough sleep, levels of the hunger hormone ghrelin rise and the satiety hormone leptin dips. This makes your body pile on belly fat, and it also makes you feel hungry, sluggish and stressed. In fact, a study at Walter Reed Army Medical Center in Washington, DC, found that people who slept fewer than 6 hours a night tended to weigh more than people who slept more – even though these sleep skimpers walked an extra 1.5 miles (2.4 km) a day. And a Harvard study of more than 68,000 women determined that those who slept 5 hours or less a night gained just over a kilo (2.5 lb) more over a 16-year period than women who regularly slept 7 hours or more.[6, 7]

9. Exercise (some).

You don't have to pump iron or run 5 miles a day to succeed on *CarbLover's*. But exercise will help you lose weight more quickly, and you'll feel great doing it, too. Now is the perfect time to get back into shape with The *CarbLover's* Workout on page 239.[8] It's an optional routine that combines strength-training and cardio, burning loads of calories in under 20 minutes! If that's too much structure for you, then try these oldies but goodies: Take the stairs instead of the lift, consider walking or biking to work rather than driving, or spend an afternoon walking with friends or your family instead of doing errands by car.

Your energy on carbs

Carbs prevent fatigue in two ways. They keep muscle glycogen levels stocked to capacity, which gives you more energy during workouts. What's more, high-Resistant Starch carbs help your body burn fat more efficiently, so you stay energized longer.

Ask the **carb pro**

Frances Largeman-Roth, RD

Q. Will exercising while on *CarbLover's* make me binge – and not lose weight?

A. No. Bottom line is that even if you feel hungrier after a workout, you're still probably burning more calories than you take in. Researchers recently studied 12 people, tracking their energy expenditure and food intake for 16 days. The participants were hungrier after they exercised, but they only compensated (by eating) for about 30 per cent of the calories burned. In other words, 70 per cent of the calories they burned during exercise stayed burned. An Australian study found that exercising made study participants feel hungrier just before meals, but they felt satisfied more quickly when they did eat. So you'll always be ahead of the game if you exercise!

"I Lost Weight on *CarbLover's*"

BEFORE

SERENA TONG

Age: 28
Height: 1.65 m (5' 5")
Weight before: 62.1 kg (9 st 11 lb)
Weight after: 57.6 kg (9 st 1 lb)
Weight lost: 4.5 kg (10 lb)

Biggest success moment: When I got on the scales and saw a sustained weight loss every week. When I had done crash diets before, I'd yo-yo, but I knew this diet was working because I consistently lost every week.

Biggest challenge: Ending my addiction to fast food. *CarbLover's* taught me to make quick meals.

Favourite recipe: Bacon, Pear & Gorgonzola Pizza (page 194). It tasted like what comes out of a delivery box!

AFTER

I started CarbLover's because I was getting married, and I wanted to look my best in my curve-hugging, trumpet-style gown. But I needed to find a diet that I could sustain beyond my honeymoon.

When I started *The CarbLover's Diet*, "starch" was a four-letter word. I've tried low-carb diets, like South Beach, before, and I kept the weight off for a month but always gained it back.

During the first phase And unlike other diets, there was a lot of real food, rather than those processed, fat-free snacks that can set you up for an afternoon meltdown. As the diet progressed, I learned that if I allowed an hour or two on Sunday night, I could prepare all my lunches for the week. Knowing that I had a stash of healthy lunches made me less stressed.

CarbLover's has taught me that eating the right types of carbohydrates is a good thing for my body. Finally, I've found a diet that controls my stress-eating, doesn't make me feel deprived, and has returned me to my "happy weight".

PART

3

Eat Carbs, Stay Slim— For Life!

Chapter 9

The *CarbLover's* Workout

GOOD NEWS: You don't have to pump iron or run marathons to succeed on *The CarbLover's Diet*. But exercise will help you lose weight more quickly (and keep it off), and you'll feel great doing it, too. That's because a diet rich in Resistant Starch and other carb foods fuels your muscles, speeds your metabolism and makes your energy soar! This three-part, full-body routine takes less than 30 minutes, and you can do it at home or at the gym. You'll burn nearly 900 extra calories a week, plus trim up to 7.5 cm (3 inches) a month from your waist, hips and thighs!

NOTE: Please get clearance from your doctor before starting The *CarbLover's* Workout, especially if you've been inactive for a while.

1. CARBLOVER'S SUPER TONE-UP!

Doing this all-over strength workout twice a week gets you extra benefits: Each move is a "compound" exercise, meaning it targets multiple muscle groups.

WORKOUT PLANNER

Do these moves with dumb-bells, a sturdy bench or step, a mat and a stability ball. Here's a sample schedule; feel free to skip a day here and there.

Monday: Cardio Interval Workout
Tuesday: *CarbLover's* **Super Tone-Up!**
Wednesday: Cardio Interval Workout
Thursday: Firm Your Tum Routine
Friday: Cardio Interval Workout
Saturday: *CarbLover's* **Super Tone-Up!**
Sunday: Cardio Interval Workout

Squat To Overhead Press

for quadriceps, hamstrings, bum, abs, shoulders

A. Stand with feet shoulder-width apart, elbows bent, a 2 kg (5 lb) weight in each hand at shoulder height, palms forward. Lower into a squat (don't let knees go past toes); hold for a moment.

B. Push through heels to stand up, pressing weights overhead. Return to starting position. Do 3 sets of 15 reps.

Single-Leg Dumb-bell Row
for back, shoulders, biceps, abs,
quadriceps, hamstrings, bum

A. Stand holding a 2–4 kg
(5–10 lb) weight in right
hand. Hinge forward so back
is flat and almost parallel to
floor; rest left hand on a
chair or low shelf for support.
Extend right arm towards
floor, palm facing in; lift
straight right leg behind you
so body forms a T.

B. Slowly bend right elbow
and draw weight up until
elbow is even with torso; hold
for a moment, and then lower
weight. Do 15 reps, and then
switch sides and repeat.
Do 3 sets.

Step-Up With Bicep Curl
for quadriceps, hamstrings, bum, abs, biceps

A. Stand with right foot on a sturdy bench or step, with a 2 kg (5 lb) weight in each hand.

B. With weight on right foot, lift to standing on the step, left thigh raised so it's parallel to floor; at the same time, curl weights up towards shoulders. Return to starting position. Do 15 reps, and then switch sides and repeat. Do 3 sets.

Superman
for back, bum

Lie face down with arms and legs extended, toes pointed, palms down. Inhale while raising arms and legs as high as you can; pause, and then exhale while slowly returning to starting position. Do 3 sets of 15 reps.

Dolphin Plank
for back, abs, shoulders

A. Lie face down with toes tucked. Keeping forearms on floor, pull belly button in towards spine and raise hips to come into low plank position.

B. Inhale while lifting hips further so body forms an inverted V; pause, and then slowly return to starting position. Do 3 sets of 15 reps.

Curtsy Lunge
for hips, bum, quadriceps, hamstrings, abs

Stand with feet hip-width apart, hands on hips. Take a giant step diagonally back with left foot and cross it behind your right; bend knees (as if curtsying) as you reach your left hand towards floor on the outside of your right foot. Return to starting position. Do 15 reps, and then switch sides and repeat. Do 3 sets.

2. FIRM YOUR TUM ROUTINE

Completing this tum-focused set will help you get flatter abs in no time. It's fine to do this series on the same day as you do the all-over tone-up routine, too.

Crunch 'n' Reach

A. Lie with your shoulder blades, back and hips on a stability ball, knees shoulder-width apart and bent to 90 degrees, feet on the floor. Extend your arms overhead.

B. Draw your lower abdomen in towards your spine. Slowly raise your arms above your shoulders while lifting your chest so that both shoulder blades and your upper back come off the ball. Hold for 3 seconds, and then return to starting position. That's 1 rep. Do 3 sets of 15 reps.

Twisting Knee Crunch

A. Lie on your back on a stability ball with feet hip-distance apart on the floor and knees bent to 90 degrees. Bring your left hand behind your head and your right fingertips to the floor for balance. Brace your core and lift your right foot off the floor. Extend your right leg, foot flexed.

B. Crunch up, twisting your left shoulder and rib cage towards your right knee while simultaneously stretching your left leg straight (keep your foot on the floor). Return to starting position (right leg lifted, left leg bent). That's 1 rep. Do 15 reps, and then switch sides and repeat. Do 3 sets.

Stir the Pot

Kneel in front of a stability ball with your forearms and elbows on the ball, hands clasped. Roll the ball forward until your legs are extended and your body is in plank position, toes tucked. Your shoulders should be stacked directly above your elbows, chest lifted off the ball, and neck in line with your spine. Brace your abs, and make small circles to the right with your forearms, as if stirring a pot. Do 15 reps, and then repeat, making circles to the left. Do 3 sets.

Figure 8 Lunge

A. Stand with your feet together, holding a stability ball in front of your body with arms bent. Step your left foot out to the side, and bend your knee to 90 degrees (don't let it go past your toes); both feet should still be facing forward. At the same time, hinge and twist at your hips to bring the ball down to the outside of your left knee.

B. As you push off with your left foot to return to starting position, lift the ball up and over your left shoulder to complete the first half of the figure 8. Repeat the lunge and ball movement on the other side to complete the figure 8; that's 1 rep. Do 3 sets of 15 reps.

3. BLAST FAT & CALORIES CARDIO INTERVAL WORKOUT:

Burn fat and stoke your metabolism by doing one of these interval workouts for 35 minutes four times per week. The intensity levels are based on a scale of 1 to 10, where 1 is not much effort and 10 is pushing as hard as you can.

Outdoor walking workout:

- Walk at an intensity of 3 to 4 for 4 minutes to warm up.
- Pick up your pace for 3 minutes so you're working at a 6 to 7.
- Crank your pace up to an 8 for 2 minutes. Take shorter, faster steps, drive your bent elbows back, and let your hips move.
- Repeat steps 2 and 3 four more times.

Treadmill workout:

- Walk at a moderate pace with no incline (an intensity of 3 to 4) for 4 minutes to warm up.
- Pick up your speed to a 6 to 7 for 3 minutes.
- Rev up your pace to an 8, and increase the incline to 2 for 2 minutes.
- Repeat steps 2 and 3 four more times.

Elliptical workout:

- Use light resistance with a medium ramp (for an intensity of 3 to 4) for 4 minutes to warm up.
- Keeping light resistance, raise ramp to high for 3 minutes, aiming for an intensity of 6 to 7.
- Lower ramp and increase resistance; work at a challenging pace (about an 8) for 2 minutes.
- Repeat steps 2 and 3 four more times.

Bike workout (outdoor or indoor):

- Pedal at medium (an intensity of 3 to 4) for 4 minutes to warm up.
- Increase your speed and/or resistance to moderate intensity (6 to 7) for 3 minutes.
- Up your intensity to an 8 for 2 minutes.
- Repeat steps 2 and 3 four more times.

"I Lost Weight on *CarbLover's*"

BEFORE

MELISSA THOMAS

Age: 27
Height: 5'8"
**Weight before: 96.2 kg
(15 st 2 lb)**
**Weight after: 89.4 kg
(14 st 1 lb)**
Weight lost: 6.8 kg (15 lb)

Biggest success moment:
Getting to a healthy weight so I can
be a healthy mum in the future.
Biggest challenge: Even with the
flexibility of *CarbLover's*, there were
still times I faced temptation. To
dodge it, I tell myself how much
exercise I'll have to do if I give in
– like, "it takes me an hour to burn
off a chocolate bar" – and most of
the time it's just not worth it.
Favourite recipe: Chocolate-
Dipped Banana Bites (page 212)
and Dark Chocolate & Oat Clusters
(page 213)!

AFTER

My husband and I hope to have a baby soon, and I want to lose weight before getting pregnant. Last year I tried and failed on two different diets: One was all about counting points (so tedious). The other was super-strict: Some days I couldn't have protein, other days I couldn't have cooked veg, and on other days I couldn't have carbs. Both diets had too many restrictions. Each time, I ended up quitting, regaining the weight I'd lost, and going back to my old clothes size.

I hoped CarbLover's would address the problem I had with other diets – and it did! It is simple, flexible and allows me to eat anything and everything I want, even crisps, chocolate and olives. When I saw the plan, I was like, "Wow ... I can have olives?" There's no one telling me I can't have something!

The recipes were easy to adapt, too. After I learned about how important Resistant Starches are, I started using them in my own recipes. For example, I added sweetcorn and black beans to my favourite turkey burger recipe.

Best of all, I'm getting the weight-loss results I want! I lost 1.8 kg (4 lb) during the first week, and after 10 weeks I'd lost 6.8 kg (15 lb). I've got about 10 kg (22 lb) to go until I reach my goal – I'm definitely sticking with *CarbLover's*!

Chapter 10

CarbLover's for Life!

YOU'VE REACHED YOUR GOAL WEIGHT, and you're feeling absolutely amazing. You're also probably feeling just a little bit nervous. That's because you've lost weight before, but then you gained back every pound, plus a few extra. NOT THIS TIME. **CarbLover's** was designed to be the diet that finally allows you to achieve permanent weight loss. And it really will work. Here's why: On **CarbLover's**, you didn't cut out anything to lose the weight, so you don't have any foods or food groups to add back in. (We didn't even ask you to give up crisps or wine or chocolate!) Nothing has been off limits during the diet, so there's no risk of you pigging out on foods you've been craving.

What's more, the dietitians who created **CarbLover's** found a sneaky way to make sure you would stay as thin as you are today. The new you has been eating the right foods in the right portions all along. Phase 2 of **The CarbLover's Diet** had you eating 1,600 calories (and your daily target of Resistant Starch-rich foods) a day, and if you're at your goal now, that's exactly the right amount to help you maintain your new smaller self.

Of course, if your jeans feel a little too tight again, go right back to Chapter 8 for quick weight-loss strategies. And if you're one of those rare, lucky people who can't stop losing weight while enjoying all the carbs you want, then go ahead – eat an extra snack or allow yourself slightly bigger portions.

Many people make the mistake of eating more or changing things up once they reach their weight-loss goal. But here's the deal: Your metabolism slows down as your body gets lighter. So you can't go back to eating what it took to maintain your weight at, say, 70 kilos – now that you weigh 60.

At the same time, now that you've tasted real weight-loss success, it's time to expand your horizons. There are steps you need to take over the next few weeks, months, even years to make a complete transition from following **The CarbLover's Diet** to living the **CarbLover's** Life. But the rules are straightforward and easy-to-follow (and you've been practising). If you follow them, you'll learn to make smart food choices automatically at your book group, on holiday, even at Christmas.

Ask the carb pro

Frances Largeman-Roth, RD

Q. How can I stay on track with *CarbLover's* when I'm juggling work, kids, the washing ... ?

A. Use the power of the Post-It to keep Resistant Starch in mind. Put notes on your fridge, mirror, dashboard, etc., with messages like "Beans are Beautiful" and "Bananas = Bikini Body".

4 CARBLOVER'S RULES IN THE KITCHEN

1. Make at least **one** meal a day that includes all of these:

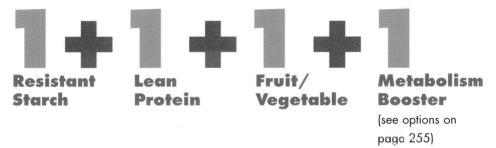

Resistant Starch **Lean Protein** **Fruit/ Vegetable** **Metabolism Booster**
(see options on page 255)

If you can't include a metabolism booster or a protein at a meal, double your serving of Resistant Starch in order to compensate. Otherwise you'll end up hungry. For the perfect **CarbLover's** portions, see the chart on pages 254–255.

2. When choosing among grains and starches, always choose Resistant Starch (see the charts on pages 254 and 264) or high-fibre carbs (see the chart on page 265) over highly refined starches such as regular pasta (made from refined flour), white rice, white bread and low-fibre breakfast cereals.

3. Choose high-performance fats such as MUFAs and omega-3s (for a list, see pages 266–267). Specifically, we're talking about avocados, olives and olive oil, fatty fish such as anchovies and salmon, peanuts, seeds and nuts, and coconut products. Use olive oil instead of other cooking oils on salads. Use guacamole or hummus as a sandwich spread in place of butter and mayo.

4. When adding flavour to various dishes, consider using a metabolism booster, such as cayenne pepper, vinegar or anchovy paste.

CARBLOVER'S PORTION SIZES

HIGH-RESISTANT STARCH CHOICES

(150 calories)

1 large banana

150 g (5 oz) barley

125g (4 oz) beans

2 slices wholemeal bread (25 g /1 oz) slices

1 wholemeal English muffin

25 g (1 oz) corn tortilla chips

40 g (1½ oz) cornflakes

25 g (1 oz) puffed wheat

150 ml (5 fl oz) cooked polenta

4 crispbreads

100 g (3½ oz) cooked lentils

100 g (3½ oz) cooked millet

150 g (5 oz) cooked brown rice

50 g (2 oz) oats, uncooked

150 g (5 oz) cooked wholewheat pasta

150 g (5 oz) cooked peas

2 small pittas

100 g (3 ½ oz) plantain

25 g (1 oz) popped popcorn

1 ounce potato chips

1 small potato, baked

150 g (5 oz) potatoes, cooked and cooled

15 cm (6-inch) tortillas

150 g (5 oz) cooked cubed yams

LEAN PROTEIN CHOICES (COOKED PORTION)

(150 calories)

75 g (3 oz) skinless poultry

75 g (3 oz) fish (especially salmon)

50 g (2 oz) lean beef

75 g (3 oz) soya beans

175 g (6 oz) tofu

2 eggs

PRODUCE

**Vegetables
(unlimited, no portion
control needed!)**

Artichokes
Asparagus
Aubergine
Bean sprouts
Broccoli
Brussels sprouts
Cabbage
Carrots
Cauliflower
Celery
Courgettes
Cos lettuce
Cucumbers
Dark green leafy lettuce
Green beans
Green or red peppers
Iceberg lettuce
Kale
Mushrooms
Okra
Onions
Pak choi
Spinach
Spring greens
Tomatoes
Watercress

Fruit
Any medium whole fruit
125 g (4 oz) berries or sliced fruit

METABOLISM-BOOSTING CHOICES

(100 calories or less)

1 tbsp olive oil
2 tbsp nuts or seeds
1 tbsp peanut butter
1 tbsp almond butter
3 tbsp coconut milk
5 tbsp dessicated coconut
¼ bar chocolate
2 tbsp flaxseeds
350 ml (12 fl oz) low-fat yogurt
1 slice low-fat cheese
240 ml (8 fl oz) semi-skimmed milk
125 g (4 oz) low-fat soft cheese (ricotta, cottage, etc)
1 small whole fruit
125 g (4 oz) sliced fruit
75 g (3 oz) dried fruit

SCORE A PERFECT RS 10

All the meals in **The CarbLover's Diet** add up to at least 10 grams of fat-flushing Resistant Starch a day. But it's easy to get the Resistant Starch you need on your own! Just use the list of high-Resistant Starch carbs on page 254 along with the nutritional info with the **CarbLover's** recipes to count RS grams and make sure your own menu adds up to a slimmer you. Here's a quick RS cheat sheet.

Breakfast Carbs **+**	Lunch Carbs **+**	Dinner Carbs **=**	10+ grams of Resistant Starch per day
1 banana (4.7 g) in a smoothie	125 g (4 oz) cannellini beans (3.8 g)	1 serving wholewheat pasta (2 g)	10.5 g
1 banana (4.7 g) with porridge (0.5g)	Sandwich on rye bread (1.8 g)	100 g (3 ½ oz) brown rice (1.7 g) with 125 g (4 oz) black beans (1.5 g)	10.2 g
Cornflakes (0.9 g) with banana (4.7 g)	Ham, Sliced Pear & Swiss Sandwich (2.6 g)	75 g (3 oz) barley (1.9 g)	10.1 g
Banana & Almond Butter Toast (5.6 g)	Black Bean & Courgette Quesadillas (4.7 g)	Baked potato (1.4 g)	11.7g
Puffed wheat cereal (0.9 g)	Greek Lentil Soup with Toasted Pitta (5.3 g)	Barley Risotto Primavera (4.1 g)	10.3 g
Breakfast Barley with Banana & Sunflower Seeds (7.6 g)	Sandwich on pumpernickel bread (2.6 g) with 25 g (1 oz) potato crisps (1 g)	75 g (3 oz) millet (1.5 g)	12.7 g
Apple & Almond Muesli (4.6 g)	Potato salad (2.3 g) with salad leaves and rye crispbreads (0.8 g)	Bistro-Style Steak with New Potatoes (2.3 g)	10 g
Blueberry Oat Pancakes with Maple Yogurt (4.6 g)	Mediterranean Pasta Salad (2.4 g)	Black Bean Tacos (4.7 g)	11 g

Use Resistant Starch
ingredients like these to
build your own
CarbLover's meals!

4 STEPS TO A CARBLOVER'S RESTAURANT MEAL

1. Skip the main course. Instead, have two side dishes and one starter (see our Clip & Carry cheat sheet on the next page). That's dinner. Main courses at many restaurants offer more food than any normal human being should be eating and will probably come in at half your total calorie count for the day. By following these "side" rules, you'll stick to your diet and never feel hungry!

2. Order a **CarbLover's** starch side dish. Always swap empty-carbs side dishes (refined bread, pasta, rice) for Resistant Starch carbs, like sweetcorn and brown rice (use the lists on pages 254 and 264). If a Resistant Starch carb is not available, go for high-fibre carbs as a second option (see page 265 for a list). And take your carbs naked. That means no sauce or butter. Have baked potatoes instead of dauphinoise, brown rice instead of rice pilaf, and plain bread instead of buttered.

3. Combine your Resistant Starch side dish with a vegetable, either as a side dish (like steamed broccoli) or as a small salad. (No fattening add-ons like sour cream or fried onions!)

4. Add a starter.–Good options include: prawn cocktail, ceviche, black bean soup, turkey chilli, and prawn or chicken kebabs. Order starters baked, grilled or steamed; avoid anything that's breaded and fried, because they may not be prepared with healthy fats.

Congratulations! Start enjoying your new carb-filled life!

I am absolutely thrilled that you've embraced carbs (and CarbLover's), lost all the weight you wanted, and have reached your goal (or soon will) ... for good. Please send me an update on your fabulous new life and share photos of yourself before you started **CarbLover's** and how you look today at **carblovers@health.com**!

Before, you were probably obsessed with dieting: *Can I resist that doughnut? I'm not sure if I should eat that slice of bread. I can't have pasta!* But now, all the dieting and the hunger has finally ended, and you can allow something else to become the centre of your life. The best news of all: Now that you're eating in a way that really nourishes your whole self, you have an untapped reservoir of energy that you can apply to the rest of your life. Get out there, and enjoy every bite of it.

CLIP & CARRY
THE *CARBLOVER'S* DIET
RESTAURANT CHEAT SHEET

American
(suggested menu items to mix and match)
Baked potato + steamed asparagus + prawn cocktail
Baked sweet potato + steamed broccoli + steak skewers

Italian
(suggested menu items to mix and match)
Granary roll + basic house salad with light vinaigrette + steamed mussels
Sliced wholemeal baguette + basic house salad with light vinaigrette + grilled calamari

Indian
(suggested menu items to mix and match)
Brown rice + vegetable kebabs + chicken tikka (marinated chicken)
Roti (wholemeal bread) + vegetable kebabs + dahl (lentil stew)

Chinese/Asian
(suggested menu items to mix and match)
Brown rice + garlic sugarsnap peas + steamed prawn dumplings
Brown rice + spicy green beans + chicken lettuce wraps

Mediterranean
(suggested menu items to mix and match)
Wholemeal pitta + basic Greek salad (tomato, cucumber, onion, olives,
green pepper – easy on the feta & dressing) + hummus
Skordalia (potato-garlic dip) + basic Greek salad (tomato, cucumber, onion,
olives, green pepper – easy on the feta & dressing) + chicken satay

Mexican
(suggested menu items to mix and match)
Tortilla chips (not fried) + salsa + black bean soup
Corn tortillas + fajita-style vegetables + fajita-style chicken or steak

"I Lost Weight on *CarbLover's*"

BEFORE

CARISSA PELLETIER

Age: 34
Height: 1.8 m (5'11")
Weight before: 98.9 kg (15 st 8 lb)
Weight after: 92.5 kg (14 st 8 lb)
Weight lost: 6.4 kg (14 lb)

Biggest success moment: I'm fitting comfortably into some clothes that I could only just squeeze into before.

Biggest challenge: Not being 100 per cent supported by my friends and family who don't have to diet.

Favourite recipe: I LOVED both of the taco recipes – the Fish Tacos with Sesame-Ginger Slaw (page 172) and the Black Bean Tacos (page 104). They don't taste like diet food at all.

AFTER

I tried *CarbLover's* **because** I wasn't feeling good about my weight or myself. At 98.9 kg (15 st 8 lb) (and creeping up), I reached a point where I was ready to do something about it. Other diets didn't give me enough food – I was hungry all the time. But *CarbLover's* put real food on the menu. The idea of making pasta, tacos and desserts inspired me to restock my larder and fridge and actually plan meals. Have you ever heard of anyone being excited about cooking on a diet? Well I was. The CarbLover's recipes were easy and delicious!

I wasn't surprised to lose 1.8 kg (4 lb) in my first week – but I was surprised that I did it without starving myself! The wholesome carbs and Resistant Starch are as filling and satisfying as promised. Once I learned the principles of *CarbLover's,* I used them to tweak my own favourite recipes. For example, I cook with more wholewheat pasta now – I use it to make linguine with clam sauce. I also changed the way I order in restaurants: I ask for more vegetables and try to swap brown rice for white when we go for Chinese food.

After 12 weeks, my weight loss has slowed down, but I am a whole size smaller than I was when I first began *CarbLover's.* I'm planning a trip to Aruba in a few months, and with the weight I've lost, I'm going to reward myself by buying a new, smaller swimsuit for that trip!

Chapter 11

The *CarbLover's* Ultimate Eat-Out Guide

IN THIS CHAPTER, you'll get even more support to help you follow *The CarbLover's Diet* no matter where you are. We've given lists of the top foods for Resistant Starch and also for foods that are high in fibre, monounsaturated fatty acids (MUFAs) and omega-3s. You'll even find the right foods in the right portion sizes so you don't have to do the sums yourself.

TOP RESISTANT STARCH FOODS

Food	Calories	Serving Size	Grams
Banana, green	105	1 medium (18–20 cm/7-8")	12.5g
Banana, ripe	105	1 medium (18–20 cm7-8")	4.7g
Oats, dry/cooked	153	50 g (2 oz)	4.6g
Beans, cannellini, cooked/canned	124	125 g (4 oz)	3.8g
Lentils, cooked	115	100 g (3½ oz)	3.4g
Potatoes, cooked & cooled	118	1 potato; 6 cm (2.5") diam.	3.2g
Plantain, cooked	89	75 g (3 oz)	2.7g
Chickpeas, cooked/canned	143	½ cup	2.1g
Pasta, wholewheat, cooked	174	1 cup	2.0g
Barley, pearl, cooked	97	75 g (3 oz)	1.9g
Pasta, white, cooked & cooled	221	150 g (5 oz)	1.9g
Beans, kidney, cooked/canned	112	125 g (4 oz)	1.8g
Potatoes, boiled (skin & flesh)	118	1 potato	1.8g
Rice, brown, cooked	109	100 g (3 ½ oz)	1.7g
Beans, pinto, cooked/canned	122	125 g (4 oz)	1.6g
Peas, vegetable/canned/frozen	62	75 g (3 oz)	1.6g
Pasta, white, cooked	221	150 g (5 oz)	1.5g
Beans, black, cooked/canned	114	125 g (4 oz)	1.5g
Millet, cooked	104	75 g (3 oz)	1.5g
Potatoes, baked (skin & flesh)	130	1 small	1.4g
Bread, pumpernickel	71	1 oz (25 g) slice	1.3g
Polenta, cooked	113	8 tablespoons	1.0g
Yam, cooked	79	100 g (3½ oz)	1.0g
Potato crisps	158	25 g (1 oz)	1.0g
Cornflakes	100	25 g (1 oz)	0.9g
Bread, rye (whole)	73	25 g (1 oz) slice	0.9g
Puffed wheat	55	15 g (½ oz)	0.9g
Crackers, rye	101	8 tablespoons crushed	0.8g
Tortillas, corn	62	25 g (1 oz) 15 cm (6") tortilla	0.8g
English muffin	134	1 whole muffin	0.7g
Bread, sourdough	82	25 g (1 oz) slice "small"	0.6g
Crackers, rye	73	2 crispbreads	0.6g
Porridge, cooked	166	240 ml (8 fl oz)	0.5g
Bread, Italian	77	25 g (1 oz) slice	0.3g
Bread, wholegrain	75	25 g (1 oz) slice	0.3g
Corn chips	147	25 g (1 oz)	0.2g
Crispbread (Melba toast)	64	½ cup rounds	0.2g

TOP FIBRE FOODS

The following foods are all naturally rich in fibre. Both the calorie and fibre amounts are given per 240 ml (8 fl oz).

Food	Calories	Grams of Fibre
Artichokes	76	14g
Barley, pearl, cooked	193	6.0g
Beans, baked, canned	368	10g
Beans, black, cooked	228	15g
Beans, kidney, cooked	225	11g
Beans, pinto, cooked	244	15g
Beans, navy, cooked	255	19g
Beans, cannellini, cooked	299	13g
Buckwheat flour, whole-groat	402	12g
Bulgur, cooked	151	8g
Chickpeas, cooked	268	13g
Dates, chopped	415	12g
Lentils, cooked, boiled, without salt	230	16g
Oat bran, raw	231	15g
Peas, split, cooked	231	16g
Raspberries, frozen	64	11 g
Refried beans, canned, vegetarian	201	11 g
Soup, bean with ham, canned, chunky, ready-to-serve	231	11g
Wheat flour, wholemeal	407	15g

TOP MONOUNSATURATED FATTY ACIDS (MUFAs) FOODS

These foods are all naturally rich in MUFAs.

Food	Calories	Serving Size	MUFA
Avocados	322	1 avocado	20g
Macadamia nuts, dry roasted	203	25 g (1 oz) (10-12 nuts)	16.8g
Plain chocolate chips	806	175 g (6 oz)	16.7g
Hazelnuts	178	25 g (1 oz) (21 nuts)	12.9g
Pecans	196	25 g (1 oz) (20 halves)	11.6g
Pork, spare ribs	314	3 oz	11.4g
Lamb, chops	305	3 oz	10.6g
Olive oil	119	1 tbsp	9.9g
Ricotta cheese	428	250 g (8 oz)	8.9g
Rapeseed oil	124	1 tbsp	8.9g
Almonds	163	25 g (1 oz) (23 nuts)	8.8g
Salmon	335	½ fillet	8.2g
Cashews	163	25 g (1 oz)	7.7g
Peanuts	166	25 g (1 oz) (approx 28)	7.4g
Brazil nuts	186	25 g (1 oz) (6-8 nuts)	7.0g
Pistachios	162	25 g (1 oz) (49 nuts)	6.9g
Sunflower seed kernels	186	4 tablespoons	3.0g

TOP OMEGA-3 FOODS

These are the planet's richest foods in omega-3s, ranked from most to least.

Food	Calories	Serving Size	MUFA
Walnuts	185	25 g (1 oz)	2.6g
Mackerel, canned, drained	177	125 g (4 oz)	1.5g
Salmon	184	75 g (3 oz)	1.2g
Tuna, canned	109	75 g (3 oz)	0.7g
Fish, herring, kippers	62	25 g (1 oz)	0.6g
Anchovies	60	25 g (1 oz)	0.6g
Pollock	100	75 g (3 oz)	0.5g
Plaice	99	75 g (3 oz)	0.5g
Clams	126	75 g (3 oz)	0.3g
Prawns	84	75 g (3 oz)	0.3g
Haddock	95	75 g (3 oz)	0.2g
Cod	89	75 g (3 oz)	0.1g

Ask the carb pro

Frances Largeman-Roth, RD

Q. Should I spread the word about carbs?

A. I like to think of carbs as my secret weapon. Wonder Woman's secret weapons are her indestructible bracelets and her lasso of truth. Mine is Resistant Starch. It can be your secret weapon, too! It's up to you whether you generously share it with friends or keep it to yourself. Either way, high-Resistant Starch carbs like bananas and oats are your fabulous secret to fitting into that little black dress.

"I Lost Weight on *CarbLover's*"

BEFORE

JENNIFER BERTSCH

Age: 38
Height: 1.65 m (5' 5")
Weight before: 88.5 kg (13 st 13 lb)
Weight after: 86.2 kg (13 st 8 lb)
Weight lost: 2.3 kg (5 lb)

Biggest success moment: Losing 1.4 kg (3 lb) in the first week, without feeling hungry.
Biggest challenge: Trying to convince my husband to eat the wholegrains on *CarbLover's* was tricky!
Favourite recipe: Seared Chicken Breasts with French Potato Salad (page 185). It's ready in 35 minutes, and it is something my husband and I enjoy after work.

AFTER

Even though I've always loved to cook – I trained as a pastry chef – my weight was under control until I moved from Montana to New York City. Working more than 40 hours a week made it harder to sneak in workouts, and the pounds quickly piled on. I have high blood pressure, and I knew, for my heart's sake, that I needed to clean up my diet. Of course, I wouldn't mind fitting into a size 12 again!

The emphasis on fresh food is what attracted me to *The CarbLover's Diet*. I knew I could stick to it because it focused on high-quality foods, like complex carbohydrates and fresh produce. It was also easy to adapt *CarbLover's* to my tastes. For example, I couldn't eat a whole banana in one sitting, so I began baking banana bread, using wholemeal flour and natural sweeteners like honey. When we weren't in the mood for wholegrain products and fish, I substituted roasted, skinless chicken for shellfish, and snuck in sweet potatoes as a side dish.

Unlike other diets, I didn't feel that I was missing out on my favourite foods, and my energy levels were high enough to make me feel up for training for a 10K run. Though my weight loss has been slow and steady, I know that if I continue on *CarbLover's*, I'll be able to enjoy gourmet flavours while watching the pounds drop off.

ENDNOTES

CHAPTER 1

[1]Janine A. Higgins and others, "Resistant Starch Consumption Promotes Lipid Oxidation", **Nutrition & Metabolism,** 1, no. 8 (2004): 1-11.

[2]Janine A. Higgins, "Resistant Starch: Metabolic Effects and Potential Health Benefits", **Journal of AOAC International** 87, no. 3 (2004): 761-768.

[3]"Dietary Resistant Starch Increases Hypothalamic POMC Expression in Rats", **Obesity,** (Oct. 23, 2008): 1-9, doi:10.1038/oby.2008.483.

[4]Michael J. Keenan and others, "Effects of Resistant Starch, a Non-Digestible Fermentable Fiber, on Reducing Body Fat", **Obesity,** 14, no. 9 (2006): 1523-1534.

[5]Anwar T. Merchant and others, "Carbohydrate Intake and Overweight and Obesity among Healthy Adults", **Journal of the American Dietetic Association,** 109 (2009): 1165-1172.

[6]Mary M. Murphy, Judith Spungen Douglass, and Anne Birkett, "Resistant Starch Intakes in the United States", **Journal of the American Dietetic Association,** 108 (2008): 67-78.

CHAPTER 2

[1]Grant D. Brinkworth and others, "Long-Term Effects of a Very Low-Carbohydrate Diet and a Low-Fat Diet on Mood and Cognitive Function", **Archives of Internal Medicine,** 169, no. 20 (2009): 1873-1880.

[2]Jennifer S. Coelho, Janet Polivy, and C. Peter Herman, "Selective Carbohydrate or Protein Restriction: Effects on Subsequent Food Intake and Cravings", **Appetite,** 47 (2006): 352-360.

[3]Ilana Greenberg and others, "Adherence and Success in Long-Term Weight Loss Diets: The Dietary Intervention Randomized Controlled Trial", **Journal of the American College of Nutrition,** 28, no. 2 (2009): 159-169.

[4]William S. Yancy Jr. and others, "A Low-Carbohydrate, Ketogentic Diet versus a Low-Fat Diet to Treat Obesity and Hyperlipidemia", **Annals of Internal Medicine,** 140 (2004): 769-777.

[5]Jennifer S. Coelho, Janet Polivy and C. Peter Herman, "Selective Carbohydrate or Protein Restriction: Effects on Subsequent Food Intake and Cravings", **Appetite,** 47 (2006): 352-360.

[6]Anwar T. Merchant and others, "Carbohydrate Intake and Overweight and Obesity among Healthy Adults", **Journal of the American Dietetic Association,** 109 (2009): 1165-1172.

[7]C. L. Bodinham, G. S. Frost and M. D. Robertson, "The Acute Effects of Resistant Starch on Appetite and Satiety", **Proceedings of the Nutrition Society,** 67 (May 2008): E157. Presented at the joint meeting of the Société Francaise de Nutrition and The Nutrition Society, 6-7 December 2007.

[8]Janine A. Higgins, "Resistant Starch: Metabolic Effects and Potential Health Benefits", **Journal of AOAC International** 87, no. 3 (2004): 761-768.

[9]Po-Wah So and others, "Impact of Resistant Starch on Body Fat Patterning and Central Appetite Regulation," **PLoS ONE,** 2, no. 12 (2007), http://www.plosone.org/article/info%3Adoi%2F10.1371%2Fjournal.pone.0001309.

[10]Po-Wah So and others, "Impact of Resistant Starch on Body Fat Patterning and Central Appetite Regulation", **PLoS ONE,** 2, no. 12 (2007), http://www.plosone.org/article/info%3Adoi%2F10.1371%2Fjournal.pone.0001309.

[11]Po-Wah So and others, "Impact of Resistant Starch on Body Fat Patterning and Central Appetite Regulation", **PLoS ONE,** 2, no. 12 (2007), http://www.plosone.org/article/info%3Adoi%2F10.1371%2Fjournal.pone.0001309.

[12]Janine A. Higgins and others, "Resistant Starch Consumption Promotes Lipid Oxidation", **Nutrition & Metabolism,** 1, no. 8 (2004): 1-11.

[13]Mary M. Murphy, Judith Spungen Douglass, and Anne Birkett, "Resistant Starch Intakes in the United States", **Journal of the American Dietetic Association,** 108 (2008): 67-78.

CHAPTER 3

[1]A. J. Hill and others, "Oral Administration of Proteinase Inhibitor II from Potatoes Reduces Energy Intake in Man", **Physiology and Behavior,** 48, no. 2 (1990): 241-6.

[2]L. A. Tucker and K. S. Thomas, "Increasing Total Fiber Intake Reduces Risk of Weight and Fat Gains in Women", **The Journal of Nutrition,** 139, no. 3 (2009): 576-581.

[3]Iris Shai and others, "Weight Loss with a Low-Carbohydrate, Mediterranean, or Low-Fat Diet", **The New England Journal of Medicine,** 259 (June 17, 2008): 229-241.

[4]Nicola M. McKeown and others, "Whole-Grain Intake and Cereal Fiber Are Associated with Lower Abdominal Adiposity in Older Adults", **The Journal of Nutrition,** 139, no. 10 (2009): 1950-1955.

[5]Morvarid Kabir and others, "Treatment for 2 mo with n-3 Polyunsaturated Fatty Acids Reduces Adiposity and Some Atherogenic Factors but Does Not Improve Insulin Sensitivity in Women with Type 2 Diabetes: A Randomized Controlled Study", **American Journal of Clinical Nutrition,** 86 (2007): 1670-1679.

[6]Lone G. Rasmussen and others, "Effect on 24-h Energy Expenditure of a Moderate-Fat Diet in Monounsaturated Fatty Acids Compared with That of a Low-Fat, Carbohydrate-Rich Diet: A 6 mo Controlled Dietary Intervention Trial", **American Journal of Clinical Nutrition,** 85, no. 4 (2007): 1014-1022.

[7]Juan A. Paniagua and others, "Monounsaturated Fat-Rich Diet Prevents Central Body Fat Distribution and Decreases Postprandial Adiponectin Expression Induced by a Carbohydrate-Rich Diet in Insulin-Resistant Subjects", **Diabetes Care,** 30, no. 7 (2007): 1717-1723.

[8]Carol S. Johnston, "Strategies for Healthy Weight Loss: From Vitamin C to the Glycemic Response", **Journal of the American College of Nutrition,** 24, no. 3 (2005): 158-165.

[9]Y. Wang and P. Jones, "Dietary Conjugated Linoleic Acid and Body Composition", **American Journal of Clinical Nutrition,** 79 (2004): 1153S-1158S.

[10]L. E. Norris and others, "Comparison of Dietary Conjugated Linoleic Acid with Safflower Oil on Body Composition in Obese Postmenopausal Women with Type 2 Diabetes Mellitus", **American Journal of Clinical Nutrition,** 90, no. 3 (2009): 468-476.

[11]R. N. Close and others, "Conjugated Linoleic Acid Supplementation Alters the 6 mo Change in Fat Oxidation During Sleep", **American Journal of Clinical Nutrition,** 86 (2007): 797-804.

[12]M. B. Zemel and others, "Dairy Augmentation of Total and Central Fat Loss in Obese Subjects", **International Journal of Obesity,** 29, vol. 4 (2005): 391-397.

CHAPTER 5

[1]L. E. Burke and others, "Using Instrumental Paper Diaries to Document Self-Monitoring Patterns in Weight Loss", **Contemporary Clinical Trials,** 29, no. 2 (2008): 182-193.

[2]L. E. Burke and others, "SMART Trial: A Randomized Controlled Clinical Trial of Self-Monitoring in Behavioral Weight Management-Design and Baseline Findings", **Contemporary Clinical Trials,** 30, no. 6 (2009): 540-551.

CHAPTER 7

[1]Yanni Papanikolaou and Victor L. Fulgoni, "Bean Consumption Is Associated with Greater Nutrient Intake, Reduced Systolic Blood Pressure, Lower Body Weight, and a Smaller Waist Circumference in Adults: Results from the National Health and Nutrition Examination Survey 1999-2002", **Journal of the American College of Nutrition,** 27, no. 5 (2008): 569-576.

[2]A. J. Hill and others, "Oral Administration of Proteinase Inhibitor II from Potatoes Reduces Energy Intake in Man", **Physiology and Behavior,** 48, no. 2 (1990):241-246.

[3]N. Schroeder and others, "Influence of Whole Grain Barley, Whole Grain Wheat, and Refined Rice-Based Foods on Short-Term Satiety and Energy Intake", **Appetite,** 53, no. 5 (2009): 363-369.

[4]Leonora N. Panlasigui and Lilian U. Thompson, "Blood Glucose Lowering Effects of Brown Rice in Normal and Diabetic Subjects", **International Journal of Food Science and Nutrition,** 57, no. 3-4 (2006): 151-158.

[5]Jung Yun Kim and others, "Meal Replacement with Mixed Rice Is More Effective than White Rice in Weight Control, While Improving Antioxidant Enzyme Activity in Obese Women", **Nutrition Research,** 28, no. 2 (2008): 66-71.

CHAPTER 8

[1]Barbara E. Kahn and Brian Wansink, "The Influence of Assortment Structure on Perceived Variety and Consumption Quantities", **Journal of Consumer Research,** 30, no. 4 (2004): 519.

[2]Mary M. Murphy, Judith Spungen Douglass, and Anne Birkett, "Resistant Starch Intakes in the United States", **Journal of the American Dietetic Association,** 108 (2008): 67-78.

[3]Snitker S, Fujishima Y, Shen H, Ott S, Pi-Sunyer X, Furuhata Y, Sato H, Takahashi M, "Effects of novel capsinoid treatment on fatness and energy metabolism in humans: possible pharmacogenetic implications", **American Journal of Clinical Nutrition**, 89 (2009): 45-50.

[4]M. S. Westerterp-Plantenga, M. P. Lejeune, E. M. Kovacs, "Body Weight Loss and Weight Maintenance in Relations to Habitual Caffeine Intake and Green Tea Supplementation", **Obesity Research,** 13, no. 7 (2005): 1195-1204.

[5]Michelle C. Venables and others, "Green Tea Extract Ingestion, Fat Oxidation, and Glucose Tolerance in Healthy Humans", **American Journal of Clinical Nutrition**, 87, no. 3 (2008): 778-784.

[6]A. H. Eliasson and others, "Sleep Is a Critical Factor in the Maintenance of a Healthy Weight", Presented at the June 2009 SLEEP Conference.

[7]S. R. Patel and others, "Association Between Reduced Sleep and Weight Gain in Women", **American Journal of Epidemiology,** 164, no. 10 (2006): 947-954.

[8]J. E. Donnelly and others, "Appropriate Physical Activity Intervention Strategies for Weight Loss and Prevention of Weight Regain for Adults: American College of Sports Medicine Position Stand", **Medicine & Science in Sports & Exercise,** 41, no. 2 (2009): 459-471.

CONVERSION TABLES

The recipes that appear in this cookery book use metric measurements with imperial equivalents. All spoon measurements are level unless specified otherwise. The information in the following charts is provided to help cooks who prefer to measure both liquid and dry or solid ingredients by volume in cups. All equivalents are approximate.

Cup Equivalents for Different Types of Ingredients

A standard cup measure of a dry or solid ingredient will vary in weight depending on the type of ingredient. A standard cup of liquid is the same volume for any type of liquid. Use the following chart when converting grams (weight) or milliliters (volume) to standard cup measures.

Standard Cup	Fine Powder (e.g. flour)	Grain (e.g. rice)	Granular (e.g. sugar)	Liquid Solids (e.g. butter)	Liquid (e.g. milk)
1	125 g	200 g	225 g	250 g	240 ml
3/4	90 g	150 g	175 g	180 g	180 ml
2/3	80 g	125 g	150 g	160 g	150 ml
1/2	50 g	100 g	100 g	125 g	120 ml
1/3	40 g	75 g	75 g	80 g	80 ml
1/4	25 g	50 g	50 g	60 g	60 ml
1/8	15 g	25 g	25 g	35 g	30 ml

Useful Equivalents for Liquid

Ingredients by Volume

1/4 tsp				=	1 ml	
1/2 tsp				=	2 ml	
1 tsp				=	5 ml	
3 tsp	=	1 Tbsp		=	1/2 fl oz	= 15 ml
		2 Tbsp	= 1/8 cup	=	1 fl oz	= 30 ml
		4 Tbsp	= 1/4 cup	=	2 fl oz	= 60 ml
		5 1/3 Tbsp	= 1/3 cup	=	3 fl oz	= 80 ml
		8 Tbsp	= 1/2 cup	=	4 fl oz	= 120 ml
		9 Tbsp	= 2/3 cup	=	5 fl oz	= 160 ml
		12 Tbsp	= 3/4 cup	=	6 fl oz	= 180 ml
		16 Tbsp	= 1 cup	=	8 fl oz	= 240 ml
			2 1/2 cups	=	1 pint	= 480 ml
			4 cups	=	1 3/4 pints	= 1 litre

Useful Equivalents for Dry Ingredients by Weight

(To convert grams to ounces, divide the number of grams by 30.)

1 oz	=	1/16 lb	=	25 g
4 oz	=	1/4 lb	=	125 g
8 oz	=	1/2 lb	=	250 g
12 oz	=	3/4 lb	=	350 g
16 oz	=	1 lb	=	500 g

Useful Equivalents for Length

(To convert centimetres to inches, divide the number of centimetres by 2.5.)

1 in				=	2.5 cm	
6 in	=	1/2 ft		=	15 cm	
12 in	=	1 ft		=	30 cm	
36 in	=	3 ft	= 1 yd	=	90 cm	
40 in				=	100 cm	= 1 m

Useful Equivalents for Cooking/Oven Temperatures

	Fahrenheit	Celsius	Gas Mark
Freeze water	32° F	0° C	
Room temperature	68° F	20° C	
Boil water	212° F	100° C	
Bake	325° F	160° C	3
	350° F	180° C	4
	375° F	190° C	5
	400° F	200° C	6
	425° F	220° C	7
	450° F	230° C	8
Broil			Grill

The *CarbLover's* Index

RECIPE INDEX

Snacks

Desserts

SUBJECT INDEX

W

Water, 28, 52
Water retention. *See* Bloating
Website, 17
Weight, keeping it off. *See* Lifestyle
Weight gain
  post-pregnancy, 54
  yo-yo, 226, 234, 249
Weight lifting. *See* Strength training
Weight loss
  with brown rice, 153
  expected, 59, 74, 229
  with green tea, 231–232
  how to lose more quickly, 229–233
  planned before pregnancy,
    248–249
  plateau, 82
  stories (*See* Profiles of weight-loss success)
  three factors to success, 22–29
  water weight vs. fat loss, 28
Wheat. *See* Flour, wholemeal wheat; Puffed wheat
Workouts. *See* CarbLovers Workout; Exercise

Y

Yams, 33, 264
Yogurt, 224, 255